The
Woman
who Outran
the Devil

SHIRLEY BASKETT

Monarch
B O O K S

Oxford, UK, and Grand Rapids, Michigan

First published in the UK in 2005 by Monarch Books
(a publishing imprint of Lion Hudson plc),
Mayfield House, 256 Banbury Road, Oxford OX2 7DH.
Tel: +44 (0) 1865 302750   Fax: +44 (0) 1865 302757
Email: monarch@lionhudson.com
www.lionhudson.com

UK ISBN-13: 978-1-85424-704-9
ISBN-10: 1-85424-704-2

USA ISBN-13: 978-0-8254-6095-1
ISBN-10: 0-8254-6095-6

Distributed by:
UK: Marston Book Services Ltd, PO Box 269,
Abingdon, Oxon OX14 4YN;
USA: Kregel Publications, PO Box 2607,
Grand Rapids, Michigan 49501.

Unless otherwise stated, Scripture quotations are
taken from the Holy Bible, New International Version,
© 1973, 1978, 1984 by the International Bible Society.
Used by permission of Hodder and Stoughton Ltd.
All rights reserved.

British Library Cataloguing Data
A catalogue record for this book is available
from the British Library.

Contents

Dedication

For obedience to the quiet voice of God,
I dedicate this book to Geoff Day

Acknowledgements

There are too many people who come to mind as I read over
my own saga, that I would want to thank. Even my enemies
have contributed to spurring me on to a closer walk with God!
But I must thank my mother for first introducing me to Jesus.
Also, I want to thank Briar Whitehead for her fine edit which
was a worthy gift to me. When I think of others who deserve
special mention, they are all those who have loved uncondi-
tionally, such as my sister. This makes sense since Jesus said
that the sum of our lives can be judged by how we loved God
first and then others. How do I tell the many ways that Pete
has obeyed his lifelong vow, to love me as Jesus loved his fol-
lowers? He is still my best friend and the truest love of my life.
Thanks, Pete!

Part 1

Outrunning
the Devil

How easy it had been. At last after years of furtive glances, and insatiable lust, I had caught her. It had all happened so quickly. Suddenly neither of us was trapped in another relationship and the timing was right. Beautiful, mischievous Jasmine and I had been together last weekend. To me she had the perfect body and she seemed so "together" in personality. I had wanted her for so long. It was too uncanny that I should have her now.

I sat at my desk in the little suburban travel office that I was managing, thinking. I was now aware of a pattern. In my pursuit of love, I had reached a strange impasse. Up until this time, I had chased relationships for a secure and fulfilling love, finding each time that I had pursued the wind. I was at the end of my belief that there just had to be one true soulmate out there for me. My conclusion was that pleasure was the only thing worth chasing. Forget deep love; it didn't exist, apart from friendship. Lovers were prey to be hunted.

The hunted were always just out of reach. I noted, as I sat thinking, that if I became too tired of the chase, I would begin to look back to a past time, when I was in relationship with God. Then, I would sometimes say out loud to myself, "I'm going to try to get back to God." Almost immediately, I would have the prized pleasure I had been after. This is exactly what had happened with Jasmine. I had tested the theory and deliberately said the words. There was no intent behind them at all this time. I actually didn't believe getting back into relationship with God was possible for me.

As I mulled this over in my office, it dawned with a sly understanding: I had beaten the devil at his own game. From now on I was back in control. Whatever I wanted I could have, simply by saying the "magic words", and he would dance to my tune for a change.

The conquest of the weekend had astounded me. It had also confused me. Hadn't Jasmine consumed my thoughts and been the object of my desire? Then why did this all feel so empty?

Things weren't all that perfect. For one thing, I had been unable to see her without drinking first. She made me feel nervous. Partly this was due to the image that I had tried to portray to her. I had only ever approached her drunk. Deep in my mind I was afraid that if she really knew the disturbed person that I was, she would run a hundred miles. I couldn't keep up the image I had invented.

Another and worse understanding was the knowledge that I had reached this impasse. I had beaten the devil on his own path of destruction for me, but at the expense of becoming a destroyer. First I had destroyed my own hope and my own ability to love. As long as I felt nothing and had no emotion other than lust or basic hedonistic pleasure, I was safe. I couldn't afford to love. This expectancy was long dead. Even if I had Jasmine to the end of my days, I couldn't dare love her or deeply care for her. This always ended in ruin.

Now that I was a shell, refilled with deadly, cold, selfish motives, I drew others to me. I could see them attracted to me like moths to the light, younger girls, women who still had dreams of finding love. I could do nothing but destroy them as I had been destroyed. This gave me no gratification. I already had a pact with myself that I wouldn't convert a "straight" woman to my lifestyle. I kept in mind that it was bad enough to do evil, but to teach it was worthy of far worse punishment.[1]

Now that I had become a destroyer, it appalled me how many straight women were amongst those who would offer themselves, workmates, women in pubs, casual acquaintances. I knew the mystique, the lie running underneath this, that another woman would understand and love them more than a man might.

Maybe for some of my gay friends, the power of winning people over was enjoyable. Having known God, this new state I found myself in as a love-slaughterer, made me a little afraid, even if I was presently only targeting the "converted". I was still aware that the pieces on the chessboard of the world played to a celestial audience. There would still be a final scene, a checkmate where the winning side was already decided. I had no doubt that at this stage in my life, I was a pawn in the wrong army. The devil was designing the moves.

I had won a chance to challenge check! But my opponent was still thinking. He didn't own the game anyway. I couldn't get off this lesbian playing board; I had already tried that.

All I could do was resign myself to shallow pleasure, or in cold blood decide to die. It was reasonable to consider this. At least this way I could tip the whole board out, players and all.

After eight years in the lesbian lifestyle, I could see my days were fast drawing to a dark night. I was 28 and life would be closing down once I hit 30. If I could attach myself to a compromised relationship of convenience, perhaps I could live out my days in some sort of happiness. Yet I knew that finding this person would be less than guaranteed. I had been trying for a number of years already. The other option was to do as some of my older friends had done, find a little place to live in and resign myself to an old age alone. Perhaps I could determine to drink myself to death. I'd seen a few do this. It wasn't very attractive.

My scene was a party scene. We had little care for causes or changing society. The feminists had that passion. They were like bitter cousins who sometimes came to our drinking binges, but preferred to gather in like-minded groups to concentrate on bigger issues. How to take revenge on all men whatever their perceived offences, or how to force acceptance for lesbians into mainstream society.

I went to some meetings. These women scared me; they were so full of hatred. I remember one spirited speech about how we would do the world a favour if we just killed one man a day. I couldn't help but note that the speaker had her trusty male dog with her and I had considered starting that night with an animal sacrifice. Being in terror of this woman, I would not have dared to defend even her own father, had he been the first victim.

My friends and I did what we always did. We left the meeting and went back to the "club". Here we could ignore any vitriolic talk apart from the usual fights over the pool table. This was fighting that we could understand. It was acceptable brawling. Besides at the club I could drink.

I was quite proud of my ability with the bottle. I used to use the old slogan "I'd rather have a bottle in front of me than a frontal lobotomy." Little gave me as much fun as drinking some poor average male under the table. For many years now my heroics with drinking had impressed mostly me. The outsider saw an incorrigible drunk, a foul-mouthed woman who staggered from one drink to the next. No degradation was low enough. Drunks accepted this; it was part of the lifestyle. I had few luxuries, because I never had any money and life was lived for the next party.

At the time I met Jasmine the drinking was taking a new course. Now, sometimes, it took little for me to be drunk. I was starting to handle drink badly. If I didn't drink my hands shook. I couldn't eat with anyone without nervous twitches. I simply couldn't get my fork or spoon to my mouth without tremors.

Working with customers, I would have to hold the side of the chair with one hand, letting the pressure of my fingers become white around the chair, to keep my other hand steady to write or use the phone. I was already stealing Valium from my mother's medical cabinet and combining it with drink was becoming habit.

I went to a psychologist for a year to try to discover what was making me shake. She dug out my relationship with my parents, my brother's death and drew from me everything that I had already psychoanalyzed for myself. She never once asked me about my drinking habits. In the end she came to the conclusion that my problems all stemmed from my repressive earlier beliefs in Christianity. If I could just accept myself as a lesbian I would stop swimming against the flow. If I could get rid of these primary self-condemning concepts about a God, then all would be fine.

Years later as the effects of drink and drugs wore off and my nervous system began to strengthen, I looked back at this well-meaning therapy and wondered why the repressive dogmatic beliefs of so called "liberal thinking" are so widely applauded. I grew up embracing this thinking along with the supposed "repressive" Christian thinking. My father had explored psychology, philosophy and much of what is now New Age, for answers. He was practising yoga when most New Zealanders would have thought this was some sort of milk-based dessert. I had read so much Freud and Jung that I could have psychobabbled myself into oblivion; but I still shook.

One time early in my degeneration, I had made an attempt to try to get back to God. I had gone to stay with an old Bible class teacher whose husband was a medical doctor. While I was there for the weekend, pouring out my behavioural symptoms, the doctor asked me, "Do you have a drinking problem?"

"No," I replied, puzzled. Of course I didn't have a drinking problem. I didn't drink every day!

After this I would often hear his voice saying in my mind, "Do you have a drinking problem?"

By the time I had filled in a questionnaire in a magazine and had scored about 19 out of 20, I had a reasonable idea that maybe I had a drinking problem. I wasn't totally convinced however. I knew that spirits were a problem to me. I had several times drunk a bottle of vodka or rum neat. But after twice coming close to killing myself, through drink combinations and the consequent alcohol poisoning, I had stopped drinking spirits. Besides when I did drink spirits I was vicious. I would get enraged and take on people in a fight. I couldn't fight so I would come off the worse. Cars were easier to damage and they didn't punch back.

Now I stuck to beer and wine, mostly beer. I even had a metal detachable handle that I could carry in my pocket, so that I could clip it on to a can to use anywhere. This way I didn't have to have the discomfort of the cold can in my hand. My elbow almost had a permanent crook from my hobby. As for quantity, a crate was no problem. A flagon of wine could put me out of work for a day; maybe.

Marijuana was my other poison. Lots of it and a constant stream if I could get it for nothing. For some reason I was always able to. I smoked few cigarettes during the day, but when I drank I smoked a lot and whatever I could smoke – I smoked. I smoked a pipe as well and this was for both tobacco and dope. A humble corn pipe for home, a Doctor John for outings. This was all part of my strange self-image.

Sometimes I would wear the rough clothes of the stereotype butch personality, jeans, scruffy shirts and boots. Sometimes I would wear a long gown and make-up to the club just to show off, in a sort of warped view of going in drag. To work I wore office clothes, dresses and skirts. I was as comfortable in these clothes, blending into the majority of society, as I was dressing to enjoy my personal life. Although most of my friends tended to wear jeans and shirts, and dress in a more masculine style, very few could be labelled "butch". The stereotype of the butch/fem couple didn't seem to hold in the life I led. All sorts of couples mixed and matched.

But they often had characteristics in common such as possessiveness, insecurity, jealousies, promiscuity and drink. In Sydney I lived in a different scene. There in my set, the girls were not possessive and few formed lasting relationships. It was there that I had learned to forget looking for love. There was only the pursuit of pleasure. There, I discovered the safety of casual connections: no strings and no possibilities of heart-break. Some of my friends in Sydney were bisexual. This I couldn't understand. By now the thought of sex with a male was so gross that I would squirm at the notion. Even a male leaving the toilet seat up in my flat made me feel quite ill.

Over the years, the devil had organized my liaisons well. Each one to do a little more damage than the last. Well, now he could leave me alone; I had earned my pay. The wages of sin were death.[2] I was dead, dead to love. This was the reward of poisoned sweets, made with just enough sugar coating to keep me putting them in my mouth. Now that I was dead emotionally and probably spiritually, he could find some other victim.

As I worked through my thoughts, I knew that putting any hope in a long-term relationship with Jasmine was out of the question. I would continue in my safe zone, holding onto this new lover, but actively continuing with the two others I had. There could be new conquests to add to my belt. I had to remain open. At least I knew the secret to keeping on winning the game.

Chapter 2

It was the 1950s and the Second World War was over. My father had returned from service at the front lines in Egypt and Italy. He had been an orderly in the medical corps for four years. Like so many other young soldiers, he returned, married and settled down to raise a family.

He had become a Christian when he was 17 years old and had been grateful to leave a childhood of being shunted between aunts and nearly dying of malnutrition before the age of seven. His mother was too consumed with her parties and neglected his care. My father's nickname as a boy was "Bones" and he retained a bony stature all his life. His Christian faith had survived the war, although he had been perplexed by many things that he observed in Europe.

He had been in a poor Italian village where the local church had lost its golden doors to thieves and the priests were pressuring the half-starved population to fund the restoration of the doors. As they swept out of the comfort of their quarters in their lavish robes, they bypassed starving beggars on the church steps on their mission to replace the golden doors.

He had nursed dying German soldiers: good men, family men, with belts that had inscribed on them *Gott mit uns* – God with us. These men believed that they were fighting on the side of the Christian God, just as my father did.

The first child in our family was a boy. He was quick to learn and was talking and developing well. A second child, a girl, followed two years later. Then when my brother was around four years old, he began to regress. He stopped talking and began to develop confusing traits. About this time, I was conceived. A new baby was the last thing that my parents wanted as they soon discovered the heartbreak of rearing a boy with severe autism, not that the medical world could even define it with a name at this time.

My mother often commented that it was fortunate that I was an independent baby as she had little time to coddle me. She could provide the mere basics for survival but she was preoccupied with trying to raise my increasingly difficult brother. So little was known about autism in those days. Ronnie's behaviour was unpredictable and soon he was running away, only to be returned home by the police. She had to keep her eye on him at all times.

Going out was an ordeal. He would be fine, then we would all be given an ice cream and he would react as if he had been given a burning lump of wood. He would throw himself to the ground and scream. Other mothers would come by and, with disdain, admonish my mother that *they* would discipline such a badly behaved boy! Other times, he could have his hand on a hot element and be totally oblivious.

Yet, my mother's heartache was my joy. Because my brother was home and perhaps because I could relate to him with my infant mind, I adored him. He would stick close to me and I somehow instinctively nurtured him. In some ways, I think I bonded to him instead of my remote and stressed mother.

My father's faith was suffering terrible blows through this time. Christians called around wanting to know why my father and mother weren't coming to church together. When my parents explained that it was impossible to take my brother, the visitors suggested babysitters, but none of them had the confidence or will to look after him and they were too busy doing church work.

Others came and wanted to know what secret sins my parents were harbouring to have such a child. Others explained that my brother had a demon, and left disgusted. Some believed he should be healed but could see that my parents obviously lacked faith, though their own faith never seemed to be in question.

My mother retained her ingrained, unswerving faith in Christ, but my father began to reconsider. He couldn't let go of a deep sense that there was some higher reality, but if these Christians were the expression of Christ today, he concluded there had to be other answers.

By the time I was born he was beginning to explore the philosophies of the new German theologians and psychologists for answers. He took an interest in yoga to try to quell his own torments and despair. So I grew up with a mother who held to a faith where fundamental theology was never questioned and a father who questioned everything. Emotionally my mother had enormous questions of God.

When I was four my brother had become too difficult to look after. So many friends and advisors had put pressure on my parents to put my brother away into an institute, but they had tenaciously held on to him, hoping against hope for an answer from God to heal him. Hoping to be able to nurture him to health, hoping for answers from the medical world. Now they realized that he was beginning to reach his teens and was physically too hard for my mother to control. He was starting to throw her across the room. He would still run away and there was my sister and me to think of as we grew up.

My sister was unhappy at school as other pupils, who taunted her about her "nutty" brother, shunned her. I was too young for school yet but my parents were well aware that I too would be victimized.

Ronnie would suddenly throw me, when I was a baby, against the garage wall and once he lifted an axe over me. These incidents were becoming frighteningly frequent.

They finally made a hard decision and had Ronnie admitted to Kingseat Psychiatric Hospital. We now went out to visit my brother every weekend. I missed him very much and looked forward to visiting him at his new home. It was set in beautiful gardens and the entrance had a long driveway with tall trees on either side. The buildings were whitewashed brick and they rambled over the sprawling country complex.

Suddenly we stopped visiting my brother. I had no idea why and kept asking when we would be seeing him. In the meantime we had shifted out into a newer suburb. My parents wanted to start over where no one would know of Ronnie. I had started school and they hoped that life could be a little more normal for their two girls.

Christmas came and I was now very insistent. When were we going to see Ronnie? Surely he was coming home for Christmas? Then one day I remember hiding in the back compartment of my father's VW beetle. I used to love to crawl into this space to wait until he was already too close to his work to turn around. Then I would pop up and he would have to take me to his shop at least until my mother could come to get me. It was a great holiday game.

This time I had popped up and was interrogating my father.

"When? When will we see Ronnie?" It had been so long. Then he told me that Ronnie was never coming home. He had drowned. He had run away one night in mid-winter from Kingseat and had been missing for three days. Finally a farmer found him washed up on his property.

For me the tragedy was compounded because everyone in the family had known since he died in July but they had kept it from me until nearly Christmas. In my childlike mind, I couldn't understand that they had decided to do this to try to keep me from hurt. To me it seemed that they had deliberately excluded me from being part of the family. I added to my conclusion the evidence that my sister and my father shared exactly the same initials. My brother and my mother had shared exactly the same initials, but my own initials were SEG – segregated! I had been earmarked from birth to be on the outside.

Whenever I looked back, the death of my brother was terrible, but the exclusion from being party to the family knowledge and passing rituals was, to me, the greater distress.

Now that he was gone, my mother knew only guilt and grief. Job's comforters reappeared to tell her that now he was dead she should be relieved! She never really recovered from losing him. His life and death would haunt her with pain and emotional torment to the end of her life.

One incident did give her some comfort. She had a very vivid dream one night in which Ronnie appeared to her dressed in shiny white clothes. He spread out his arms and said, "Mum, why are you crying? I am healed!" And he looked so radiant and so happy. She could barely believe that he was speaking.

I grew up knowing that I had been a bit of a mistake on the end of the line and without realizing it, due to all these events, I had very little connection with either parent. The closest person for me emotionally was now dead. I too mourned year by year on each anniversary and my childhood took on a morbid darkness.

At four years of age I remember I had asked my mother how I could have Jesus in my life. I recall kneeling by our old piano in the lounge and asking Jesus to come into my life. At this age it was easy to understand and trust that Jesus was now my best friend.

My mother cried a lot through my childhood. She mourned bitterly. My impression of these young days is one of unrelieved sorrow. She continued to go to church but the denomination and location changed frequently. If anyone mentioned that they knew of my brother, we would leave. I would go along under duress simply to keep my mother company. The two of us were Presbyterian, Methodist, Baptist,

Congregationalist, Salvationists or Brethren, depending on the next church we attended. I always considered this a rich smorgasbord that gave me some understanding of several Protestant faiths.

The highlight of my young years was my last year in primary school. I was tall for my age and that was the end of my growth upwards. Within two years I would be the second shortest in the class as everyone grew past me. However at ten I was strong and a tomboy. No tree was safe from my exploration. No neighbourhood boys were safe from my gang. We believed in hand to hand combat and ambushes and yodelling war cries from treetops and attacks to depose the boys from their tree houses. We never built any. The only time I ever came before a headmaster was in these years to be admonished for "beating up the boys".

Joan of Arc was my heroine and any film hero that was a spy. I imagined myself to be destined to become an espionage agent like James Bond or Modesty Blaise. I was just on the edge of Elvis worship and certainly caught Beatlemania. I had to see the black and white Beatles movie *A Hard Day's Night* six times, even though I barely understood it, but an eleven-year-old girl was supposed to learn to scream at her pop idols and this gave me the chance to practise.

I went on a school trip when I was ten. We stayed in the homes of the people in the regional town. It was very exciting and the home where I stayed had a girl my age. She was so pretty and I idolized her. When I returned home, I carved a heart into the wall in the toilet and inscribed, "I love Melanie Moore." My parents said nothing.

Chapter 3

I had a crush on one of my sister's friends from about the age of twelve. It never seemed to occur to me that this friend was a girl. At fourteen I began to get crushes on boys in my class and boys in the youth group that I was now attending. My heart was obsessed with one boy from about fourteen through to nearly sixteen. He was the star of the youth group and I was always impressed with heroes.

I saw myself as fat, pimply, awkward and talentless and I talked too much. I had frizzy hair that no one could find attractive and my breasts were too big. I would never find anyone who would want me. My best friend, Rachael, already had a boyfriend. This became a new goal. The song "Sweet sixteen and never been kissed" became a taunt in my mind. No matter what, I had to be kissed before I turned sixteen! Obvious to me was the thought that if you got to sixteen and no one had kissed you, then you must be very undesirable.

The hero in the youth group didn't show enough interest so I was becoming desperate. Unfortunately this was the dawning of the age of the hippie. It coincided with some of our Christian gatherings in city parks. We would be sitting around a guitar singing when a mass of Vietnam War protestors would invade the park. These gatherings turned into music "happenings" and orators would take to soapboxes. It was very exciting.

At first I would go hoping to talk to some of these people about Jesus. Then I started to enjoy the music, the dance and the characters that were emerging as new heroes to me. Apart from school and church, I hadn't mixed much with others. These people were interesting and colourful and the young men were suave and exciting. It wasn't long before I found that these young men were not quite as slow as the boys in the youth group were.

I managed my goal. Kissed before sixteen. Then having felt the stirring of sexual attraction it wasn't long before I had moved from this first boy to his older and worldlier-wise brother. By sixteen I had dropped out of school and moved into Mark's home. He had captured me with his swarthy looks, his long dark hair and his fluid dancing. He had trained for a short time in ballet and his passion for dance equalled mine. We thought that we were Romeo and Juliet.

My parents were horrified. This youngest daughter who had been burning with gospel fire had overnight gone wild. A once conservative girl at Bible class, she was now straggling down the main street in our city, Queen Street, in bare feet and patched jeans.

When I was fourteen, I had started going to a Baptist church with Rachael. I was baptized there and after my baptism, I used to bike to school singing in another language. I always thought that this was simply out of my imagination. It made me feel so close to Jesus. If anyone had suggested that I was speaking in tongues, I would have hotly denied it. Our church quite strongly taught that these gifts were not for today and that people who claimed to speak in tongues were deceived by the devil. I truly believed this, and continued on my merry way singing my strange language to God.

Following my baptism, I had discovered a tremendous hunger to learn about God and to devour the Bible. I went to a Bible class at the Baptist church in the morning, then would rush to a Presbyterian one up the road and would eagerly wait for the night service back at the Baptists. During the week I would go to a youth home meeting on a Thursday night, out on the streets trying to share my faith with a group on Friday nights, youth group on Saturday night and this was not enough. I took Bible memory tests and went to every meeting I could. I used to go to inner city prayer meetings to pray for people to know Jesus. I never do anything by half measures and I could have been accused of fanaticism.

Overnight I let all my ethics go. Mark was everything. In my mind I was going to marry him. He was all of 17 and had already fathered a child to someone else while he was still in school. None of this meant anything to me. He would love me for life and this love would be just as intense as it was when the romance began, forever and ever.

My parents were fooled for a time by my stories. I had never given them any cause to worry up until now, but eventually they realized that Mark's family home was more like a commune. Each parent had their separate lovers. It was a big rambling old house behind a factory area. I was commanded to come home.

My life had become incompatible with my parents. I had left school. My parents were discouraging me from going back to school. They believed I should just find work since I would only have to work until I married. That was their belief anyway. Education was unimportant: I was a girl.

My first job was with the railways but this lasted two months. When I moved into Mark's, I threw in my job as an office junior. Work was easy to come by so I would work if I needed money. I fought with my parents and I am sure half the neighbourhood was entertained with the screaming and yelling from our house.

Mark couldn't be pinned down. He had gone with his friend to see a little of the country and to be free. I was miserable at home and frightened that I was pregnant. I went for several months missing my "monthly". Then I was very ill. My sister nursed me. She later said that I had probably miscarried. I was sad and relieved. There was no way I could have had a baby. My mother would have disowned me. She had always threatened to send me away if I ever became pregnant outside of marriage.

My mother's fury over my behaviour was terrifying. I was already in awe of her when she was angry, but her disapproval and indignation was absolute. In this time at home, when my sister was gone again, the isolation and loneliness was unbearable. My sister had left home when I was eleven and she was sixteen. I was now sixteen and I too had to go for good.

I found a flat with five other girls who went to various churches and although I was a bit young, I made up the complement needed to pay for the house. I found a job in a wedding cake shop. The boss was intrusive with his sexual innuendoes and after two months I moved on to cleaning a motel nearby. Several other jobs followed, working in cafés, photo finishing where I put teeth into black and white photos of children, or spotted out bubbles from baby's mouths, or removed marks from a bride's dress.

Mark came back and wanted me to move into a flat with him. But it was too late, I was back attending church. This time I had started going to a Pentecostal church in the city with two of my flatmates.

At first I had been afraid to go. It was an Assembly of God church and I knew that these were the people who were deceived and believed in the gifts of the Holy Spirit, like tongues. At my first few meetings I was disturbed at people waving their hands in the air and the general noise. I went because these two flatmates seemed to have something that I hadn't seen in other Christians. There was a joy about them. They had something that I wanted.

Many of my friends had come from the political activism of the day. I marched in protest but really only to be part of the social scene. I had little idea of what the Vietnam War was all about. The night we all had to run from the smoke bombs outside the Hyatt Hotel, where Spiro Agnew was staying, was particularly exciting. Who cared who Spiro Agnew was? My new heroes were the leaders of the protest movement.

Almost as soon as I began to go to this church, there was something of a move to God. Suddenly young people, especially hippies, and protestors began to become Christians. My house had started to disintegrate already with the girls moving out for various reasons, so some of these new friends moved in. I was renting a huge, old, two-storied house. Soon we were having prayer meetings on Monday nights and every Monday someone else would encounter Jesus for the first time or be set free from demons.

Most had been into some sort of drug-taking and there was plenty of action as people were prayed for and the power of God would contest with demons for the lives of these new believers. There were some dramatic exorcisms and the changes in some of the people had to be seen to be believed. This was when I first understood something of the reality of a spiritual world, a world that was at war, along with gaining an appreciation for God's power.

I also heard people praying in tongues when I came to this new church. At first I was horrified, then I heard them singing in tongues. I was appalled! Why, this was what I had been doing for years! Once I calmed down, I let go of the warnings that I had heard from earlier days and started to research from the Bible for myself and began to have new understanding of God.

However, the battle with my passions remained. If only our wilfulness or character flaws could be exorcised as easily, but then we would be robots. One part of me sincerely desired to please God. The other side craved love and acceptance at any cost.

Every single new Christian male was a potential source of love for me. I fell for one after the other. Boyfriends were latched onto and my possessive, compulsive, dependent personality would drive them from me. Each rejection convinced me of my own unattractiveness.

The rejection from the last boyfriend had come with words that had seared me to the core. I was rammed into worthlessness. My sister had been living in Australia but she now returned to rescue me from the mess I had created for myself. She had become a Christian in Australia and her intervention was just at the right time.

When she found me in the house, I was 17 years old and I was in deep depression. The house had been invaded by all sorts of derelict people including drug users and as it was in my name, bills for overseas calls started coming in. No one admitted to them. Now with the help of my sister, I let the house go and moved home for a short time, to lick my wounds and gradually pay back my father, since he had bailed me out financially. The fights at home were fiercer. My new taste of independence had made me more ungracious and it was harder to accept the constraints of my parents.

My sister organized a new flat and we moved into another area close to the city. This time it was with two new Christian friends. I started night school to try to get into a fine arts school. I had always loved art but I wasn't disciplined enough and failed. I had a makeshift studio under the house of some of my new Christian friends across in another suburb. I stayed there sometimes if I was working on one of my bad paintings. Sculpture was my forte. Yet I pretended to be a painter and would smoke cigarettes one after the other, while slapping oils onto canvas.

Because most of my friends were Christians, I continued trying to pursue God. The attractions of dope lured me a little and I tried it for the first time. This was when I had also started smoking cigarettes. This helped me to fit in a bit more with the older new Christians who were struggling to stop! I was very quiet when they sat about discussing their own drug habits: I had nothing to add.

Chapter 4

The days were exciting. The church I was now attending had grown from around 400 people to 2,000 virtually overnight. In our group of friends there was always something new that God was doing. It was a strange and wonderful time and many of this group are in ministry today.

The biggest driving factor in my life was an ongoing craving for love. I found it temporarily in God, but I continued to search for it hoping for some person I could hold. God was so intangible. I wanted a God of flesh and blood. Confusion reigned much of the time in my youth and one time my sister advised me to get away for a while. On her advice and because I thought that this was exactly what God was saying, I took a bus north to the city of Whangarei. I arrived around 4am and had to fight off the amorous advances of a fat, toothless taxi driver as I tried to locate the local Assembly of God church. Eventually I phoned the pastor and he came and brought me to his home for the weekend. He and his wife listened to my declaration that I had felt God was sending me to their church.

I was convinced that I should stay in Whangarei for a time. The pastor thought that this was right and so I went to stay with one of his elders on a farm. I stayed with the McDonell family and learned to milk cows and to overcome my fear of these large, docile animals. I was nurtured and loved in their home. Despite my super-short mini-skirts and my odd city ways, these people showed me an acceptance that I hadn't known was possible in families.

In return, I experimented with cooking possum and giving them their first possum stew. Why waste anything, I argued. Possums are pests to be eradicated in New Zealand. They graciously ate the stew. Already I had learned how to scrounge food wherever it was. Once I lived for a few weeks off some wild apples from an empty section next door and bowls of seameal custard.

Listening to Pastor Thomas, the fiery Welshman that I had met on my first day in Whangarei, gave me a new fervour for God. I wanted more than anything to follow Jesus. The other main influence in these early years was a conference at which the speaker was Judson Cornwall. He had taught from the biblical book, Song of Songs. The fire of love that I could see in his teaching caught hold of me. I desired with all of my being to know Jesus like this. He awakened a new love in me. No one could ever come near the intimacy that I now wanted with Jesus. I never forgot this teaching and it held alive a light in the darkest of places in my later years.

I couldn't get work in Whangarei and I soon returned home. The rift with my parents was so complete that I couldn't entertain the thought of being at home. It seemed that nothing I could do or say or be would ever please my mother. My father had always been a remote figure, except when he was backing my mother. There was no way that I could stay.

I moved to Wellington, New Zealand's capital city. Here, I knew a few people and I could find work. Again I had recognized the quiet voice of God leading me.

At first I cleaned in a university girls' hostel. I boarded with a Maori lady and her young daughter. Once more I found an acceptance and I was living with the expectation of better days. There was another reason Wellington held hope: a young man called Greg lived here. We had a friendship that for me had slowly turned to admiration and love. It was the first time I had felt a love for a man that was pure and selfless and it had started with friendship. I had no idea whether he had any feelings for me. I hoped so. I knew he could see my adoration.

Cleaning wasn't much of a job, so I took work in the Baptist Book Centre. I worked with a wonderful woman called Mrs Wilson. She was one of the greatest influences on my life. I had a year with this godly woman who took a wild, untamed girl and taught her what it was to work in a job with integrity. She would tolerate any outfit I wore to work, mini-skirts, long hippie dresses, platform shoes, saris, whatever. But she would not tolerate anything that was un-ironed! I would be bundled into an old work smock and sent to the dry-cleaners, to have the offending item pressed.

Mrs Wilson taught me to never steal from a boss. This meant never writing a letter home in work time; that was stealing. Never using the boss's pen to write home with; this was stealing his ink. "Work as unto the Lord"[3] was her motto. And she loved me. She corrected me and she loved me. She would invite me to her home and would spoil me with breakfast in bed. I admired her and took every lesson she dealt me. She loved every person who came through that bookshop door.

She taught me how to sell too. Putting a book into someone's hand that would help them was a ministry. So many would go out of that shop having received at least five or six "blessings" when they had only come in for a birthday card!

While I was in Wellington, I clearly heard God calling me to Bible College. If he wanted me to go, then he would have to show me which one and get me in. I saw one advertised in Christchurch and applied. I knew nothing about it and they normally didn't accept people as young as I was. I was 18 by now. I didn't have the fees, but I was accepted. I didn't really want to leave Wellington because of Greg. He had his own aspirations for ministry and I might never see him again. In this case obedience to God was more important. If it were right for me to be with Greg, God would have to organize it.

I took a job at night in a Greek restaurant to save for Christchurch. I noticed that many waitresses came and went. I was the only long-term waitress. A policeman friend of mine would come in quite regularly for meals. He didn't tell me until years later that he had done this to make sure that I was OK. It was a recruiting point for a well-known brothel. The owner, knowing I worked in the Baptist Book Centre by day, had given strict instructions that I was not to be propositioned!

The owner and his brother who had a café next door would argue over whom I was to work for. These arguments would get very heated. They would try to tempt me to try Greek liqueurs. The cooks would shout in Greek and throw plates and I heard that one waitress had even had knives thrown at her, but she was tough enough to throw them back. I was trying to learn some Greek so I would quietly stand by and listen. I don't think I would have wanted to learn the words that they were shouting.

There were memorable nights such as the "fly under the steak" and the time a man had challenged the owner to try to chew on his piece of meat, since it had nearly broken his jaw. At least I was fed well.

After work at 10pm I would leave and feel like I had just finished my working day. I had. I couldn't bear going home to my flat on the street high above the city called the Terrace, where I was now living. I would go around to Vivian Street where all sorts of people gathered. My friends lived there and one of them, Marcus Arden, was starting to preach all over the country. He drew all sorts of people in the inner city. I fitted in well with the motley assortment that he collected. This was my second home.

At Vivian Street I felt acceptance again. I met many interesting people including the poet James K Baxter. As a young person, celebrities awed me. I was still susceptible to heroes and not particularly discerning.

This was my fun time. Mock battles with long-dry spaghetti lengths that stabbed and broke into a thousand pieces. Watching Marcus create soup from leftover meals and remembering not to partake. Cooking scones on the old coal range in the dining room. The floor sloped and walls leaned. There were always groups of people debating and discussing, praying or laughing.

I would stay late, walk home, and get up as late as possible and work. In the end I literally collapsed with exhaustion. A few days of sleep after being carried back to the flat, and I went back to the same routine.

Winter in Wellington – I would count the steps down from the Terrace to the Church of the Angels at the bottom, before hurrying in my platform shoes to the shelter of the city streets. Sometimes the notorious wind would blow my umbrella inside out or threaten to lift me from the side of the cliff. I would clutch the railing for my life.

My confusion about relationships and my quest for the partner for my life went on. By now I had fallen in love with Greg so utterly that I almost held him in god-like idolatry. I doubted I could ever meet his criteria as a wife but every day I loved him more. An odd thing happened with a young Christian man who had asked God if he should ask me out. He hadn't even realized at that point that I knew Greg. He felt God had clearly answered him and had said that Greg was to be my husband. I hardly dared to believe it but it fixed in my mind, "He must be the one."

But Greg was out of my reach and in the meantime there were others taking interest in me. By now there had been many boyfriends. The thrill of new romance caught me every time. I still went from relationship to relationship. I am sure that if the man I really loved had been at all interested, news of my many boyfriends would have thrown him from seeing my heart for him anyway. I wasn't logical enough to consider this at the time; a real boyfriend was worth more than an improbable dream.

Only one relationship turned fully sexual and this was close to the time that I was to go to Christchurch to the Bible College. This was the second relationship in my life where I had ended up sleeping with someone. I had failed utterly again. How I was tormented over my weak will! How could I blithely arrive at Bible College with this relationship just days behind me?

I couldn't blame my boyfriend, Brent; I was by now well aware that my own lusts knew little restraint. In my hunger for love, I would forget any higher morals. Something drove me to taste every chance for gratification. I became the aggressor and paid the price of guilt every time. Fortunately most of these encounters were tempered by my partners, who usually had more sense, or better self-images.

Just before Bible College, I boarded with a Christian family and the oldest son proposed to me within days of my moving in. I was so shocked that I actually went out with him for a short time. He was after all a youth leader and therefore must know more about God's will than I did. I had jumped out of one frying pan and into another fire of my own making as this encounter sent me running into the arms of Brent. I was good at that.

I wished I could have loved Brent, this Wellington boyfriend, as he had loved me. He was a good man and intelligent. But underlying all my relationships was always a first love for Greg.

Arriving in Bible College, I had to work through guilt and was again grateful that I wasn't pregnant! I had prayed fervently I would not be. As a Christian I didn't believe I should be sexually active, so would not have contemplated the idea of going on the pill. Yet, the consideration that I should not have allowed the relationship to go that far, escaped me in the heat of desire.

For a young girl who had a low sense of self-worth, the interest of young men, especially good-looking or talented young men, was very attractive. I had started to enjoy the flattery. The one man I really cared about remained beyond me. I could not have flirted with him anyway and when I did see him, I almost froze. I was bumbling and inept. I doubt he ever saw the true me.

All my other suitors saw a confident, flirtatious person. I had no trouble targeting and winning almost any other male I looked at. Then I hated myself because it was not them I wanted. I hated myself because it hindered my seeking of God. I hated myself because these relationships were all so superficial and self-seeking.

Christchurch would give me a fresh start. I was away from everyone. But even at the college I received four marriage proposals. There was a rule that we were to have no relationships while in college. I managed one, and deeply regretted it afterwards. It was not something that I had planned or intended. I was aggressive and would probably have thrown in the whole year, if he hadn't called it off. I was so grateful and relieved, as I didn't want to continue either. I was still in love with the same man I had been in love with all along.

Strangely enough I still considered myself to be particularly unattractive and somehow less of a "real girl" like my friends. I also lived with a belief that I had to quickly gratify any male because otherwise they would be in pain. Immediate passion was a panacea for my emptiness and feeling of worthlessness. I still believed in love, and more, that it might be possible for me, if God arranged it, to maybe win the love of my life, Greg.

Early in the college year, an elderly couple visited and ministered to the students. At the end of their teaching one of them said that God had shown them something about one of the students and that they would like to pray for this person.

They said, "This person has like a magnetic attraction to the opposite sex. You merely have to look at the opposite sex and you have them. You are constantly trapped into one relationship after the other. We would like you to stay after the meeting and we will pray for you."

My face was hibiscus pink. I was sure that the whole student body was focussed on me. I stayed behind and they prayed for me. I fell between the chairs in the lecture hall and when I got up I knew that I was free. From this day onward I never had this problem again. I wish they had been given a few more words from God. They might have saved me more future pain in other areas!

At the beginning of the year, once I had left behind the condemnation of my moral failings, I swung into self-righteousness and became very knowledgeable. Hadn't I soaked in the teaching of so many great teachers even before I came to college? There must be little that I didn't already know about God.

Then one afternoon I was asleep in my room. I was dreaming that I was at some social gathering and I was spouting off about what God thought about something, when I was suddenly interrupted by a voice. It pressed close to my ear and said, "But you don't know me!" I woke with a start and felt the breath still hot on my ear and the words still ringing loudly.

My heart beat swiftly for a while and I worried, was that God or the devil? The fact that I couldn't discern which, distressed me more. If I couldn't tell who spoke, how could I boast that I knew God? I took comfort that at least the voice didn't say, "I don't know you!"

The Bible College had many rules and they only became more stringent after many of us had bucked them. I had two friends in women's prison in Dunedin, who wrote to me, who seemed to have more freedom than we did.

College was easier for me because I was part of the "outreach team". We often went for weekends to other parts of the country or the city. Not only that, it was the year Christchurch hosted the Commonwealth Games and our church had a coffee bar in the city to reach people. I would sing there with an Anglican nun. If we were late out we would have to throw the sister over the wall and she would have to climb to her bedroom in her long robes up the fire ladder, by her window. It was not allowed, but she had a merry personality and loved the joke.

Visiting the nunnery was always interesting to me. It was a medieval sort of cloister enclosed behind high stone walls. Sometimes I would have a meal there and there was one very elderly diminutive nun who still wore the crisp white fluted wimple of a costume from an even earlier day.

When I visited I would have to wait in a small room after ringing the bell. One day I was tired of waiting and since I was wearing a long black skirt and black blouse, I took the chance, fastened my black cardigan around my head like a veil and waltzed in. The sister was mortified but I got away with it.

One Samoan nun and I would go into the walled court-yard where there was a huge, spreading, overladen mulberry tree. We would stand underneath it in the afternoon sun, gorging on the sweet luscious fruit. I thought about being a nun. The regimented life was appealing. I wouldn't have to think or take responsibility for anything. Perhaps I could consider being a novice?

I loved the college studies. Not that I was particularly studious, but I loved the teaching. I absorbed it all. It became the basis for my lifetime theology. There was only one class that I had difficulty with. Preacher's class. If I failed any class, I failed preacher's class. I was so terrified before an audience that my mind would go totally blank. I could sing in a trio, but I couldn't sing solo and I couldn't speak a word in front of a crowd. The dread of every eye looking at me alone was enough to petrify me on the spot.

Every time it was my turn, I would spend hours preparing. My time would come and I would walk shivering to the lectern. All eyes were on me. Whatever was on my mind was no longer there. I would panic and glance at my notes. What on earth could I say to these people that they didn't already know? It all looked like a pile of worthless empty words.

In the end no one wanted to put me through the horror of slinking from the front of the class back to my seat, having not uttered more than a stuttered apology. I was always excused.

I could lead people and I was already picked to be a team leader for student duties, despite the fact that I was the youngest in the college. I could direct a team one to one and organize anything, but I couldn't speak to groups. Only six people and I had stage fright. I had come to a conclusion that whatever I did, speaking in public would never be it. I hoped to be a pastor's wife. I would cook, entertain, clean, have children, maybe not sew, but speak – never!

During the year the man I adored visited Christchurch to preach at a local church. I had been sick and should have stayed home. I felt a caution to stay home. How could caution come into anything? He had contacted me to tell me he was coming. As if I would stay home! I took one of the girls from the college and we went to hear him preach. He did what he always did and singled me out in the congregation with smiles and winks. My heart melted. If he didn't have an interest in me, then I had to be going mad.

At the end of the service he stopped in the middle of his prayer time. He had asked for anyone wanting to know Jesus to come forward for prayer. A lady had come forward and was standing before him. Then he looked at me and said, "Shirley, I want you to come out here and pray for this lady to lead her to the Lord."

I rose and froze. I went to the front and took the mike. I shook, I trembled, and I looked at this man with horror and a touch of anger. In waves of fear mixed with rage, I wondered, was he testing me to see if I could assist him in ministry? I had never seen anyone do this! Or if he was trying to give me experience simply because I was in college, then he had picked an odd way to do this. If I had ever had an indication of his feelings, perhaps it might have just been possible to do what he asked. But this?

For an interminable time I stood staring incredulously at him, face flushed and aware that every other eye in the room looked on. Eventually he smiled benevolently and took the mike from me and went on with the task. I tucked my tail between my legs and led the woman out to counsel her. I could do that.

If ever public speaking had been sealed as anathema to me, this night had done it. I slapped myself emotionally. Why hadn't I obeyed the quiet prompting that had said, "Stay home?"

I joined my idol in the car as we returned to the pastor's for supper. He lightly said as I left, "Goodbye, sister."

Sister! I was furious. This was the brush-off. I had never even had the chance to say, "I love you! You stupid male!" He had never had the chance to say, "But we have always only been just friends, you foolish girl." Not even a decent argument.

I had promised I would pass on a letter from a mutual friend. I sent this the next week with a note that quoted Paul: "See what a large letter I write with my own hand"[4] and addressed it to my "brother". I licked my wounded pride as I sealed the envelope and posted it off. There was no reply. There never was. I felt a fool for having believed God was saying "Yes" to this man for me.

Chapter 5

Toward the end of the year at Bible College, I started to pray about what I should do after college. I had made enormous progress and had been part of a team ministering in different churches. The church leaders had suggested that I help establish a church in a coastal town. I wasn't sure.

As I prayed I felt that I should stay in Christchurch and I had the strong feeling that I was to go to the church where I had experienced my humiliation. I went to see the pastor and told him that I was finishing Bible College and that I would be coming to his church. I was available for Sunday school teaching or however he might use me. I had also met a pastor's daughter attending this church and we had related quite well.

I always had problems keeping my own secrets. My heart was not only on my sleeve but was quick out of my mouth too. I had told the pastor's daughter all about my hopes and dreams for Greg. She had shrugged and said she couldn't see what I saw in him. She would have no interest in him at all.

Then one night in prayer I sensed that God was saying that Greg was going to come to the very church I had decided to go to. I had never been sure if I was hearing right but I told my close friend who had been with me the night I had last seen him. Then a month or so later I heard that it was true. He was coming to this church to help in ministry.

I was elated. Then one night very soon after, I was visiting a pastor's daughter that I knew and she asked me, "Have you heard? Greg is engaged."

I was shattered. I left her flat and walked home. It must be true; pastor's daughters didn't lie. What would I do? I couldn't go to this church now. There was no way God could expect me to go to this church now! Not only was I a fool in my idol's eyes but I was a failure in my own. My whole world collapsed.

I started to seek God's will for my life. It was clear to me that he would not expect me to go to this church and face this. I had been beaten enough! If I ever had any pride, there was none left now. I fasted. I cried out. No further word came. I couldn't budge God from the original direction. But I couldn't obey it either. I wouldn't. This was my original sin, a bite of an apple that took me to hell and back.

I might never have considered the reality of being attracted to another woman, except that we had a student in the college who had come from a lesbian relationship, before she was a Christian. It was only months behind her and she talked of it constantly. It exposed my impressionable mind to an avenue that I had never explored before. I had been afraid of gay people. This girl always talked of the closeness of her relationship and how much she missed her old girlfriend. She talked of how she would buy her friend flowers and how they cared for each other. She had forgotten the reason why she had left this life. I never heard that. We talked often since this girl and I were part of the trio singing with the Anglican nun.

I was in a vacuum. My heart was still fully tied to Greg, but he was gone. Someone else had won him who had been more talented, better-looking, and more confident. There had to be someone else for me. I believed in soulmates. I believed as a Christian that there was the ONE. If Greg wasn't it, then what could I do? I doubted I could ever love another man. I had never in all my flirtations found anyone who could equal Greg. I just knew that there would never be another.

About this time I met Sharon through singing. Our outreach group would sometimes team up with another evangelistic organization to visit different towns. My group sang but had only an acoustic guitarist. Their group had a band but no singers. We would combine and it was through this that I met her. She played bass guitar. She was good. She was a cool character with a great sense of humour and I liked her straight away.

When we first met, we both had an uncanny feeling that we already knew each other. It was as if we were already close friends. At this time there was a likeness about us that others noticed too. We did look alike in some regards, yet not that alike. At times people couldn't tell us apart, or thought we were twins, yet looking back I can barely see a resemblance. We both had similar haircuts and thick wavy hair. This was about the only similarity.

Toward the end of winter our groups went to Kaikoura where picturesque mountains, powdered with snow, surrounded the bay. The air was electric with romance and charm. It was good to be away from the college and my confusion about where God wanted me. Here I could serve him and enjoy a winter paradise. Oddly, for the first time, thoughts of Greg were dim.

We set up in a local hall and held our meetings. We sang at the local hospital and visited people in their homes. Then the evening ended and we packed down to go home. In a momentary glance I turned to look at Sharon. She had her back to me but something in me snapped. I had found a new idol. This one was "safe". It was another girl and this would be an impossible fantasy to follow through with. I could pretend and live in my imaginary world and be safe.

For some reason, I had to travel back with the other group. This meant I would have to squeeze into the back seat with Sharon and spend hours pressed against her to keep warm. It was a journey of laughter and jokes and by the time I was placed outside my accommodation at the college I was infatuated.

Chapter 6

In the last week of college, the college head, Peter Morrow, prayed for the students. Peter was a picture of a modern-day prophet. He stood tall and lean and his red hair topped his gaunt face. When he twirled his long bony finger, it was as if the finger of God was punching through a point. Yet he had little pretension. Close up he looked at every student with the same love and interest. He was respected for his gift of prophecy, which had proved to me over the year to be powerful and accurate. So when he prophesied over me I listened.

Peter, in my last week, gave me a message he believed was from God: "If you don't choose to walk in God's ways, you will walk the lip of hell. You will experience things that others would never dare to do or see. However, if you choose God's will for your life, you will walk before kings and nations will come to you."

For a girl who could do nothing public, the thought of walking before kings was beyond belief. How nice that Pastor Morrow had given me a picturesque and exaggerated view of my possible future. I memorized it, as it sounded grandiose, along with another promise a visiting overseas speaker had given me, that the Lord would use me.

I had been warned. I knew God's direction for me at the end of this college year, but my answer was "No". I would find some other new "God's will". There had to be another way.

I had made up my mind not to go to the church. I had been back to the pastor to tell him I wasn't coming after all. I had hoped he would ask why or try to convince me otherwise, but he just accepted it. No one else could walk my walk of obedience with God for me.

My course was set. I would go and spend three days with my now good friend Sharon before leaving to return home to Auckland for a time. I could put the whole embarrassing episode of Greg behind me and find whoever it was that God must have for me. Never would I darken the doorstep of THAT church again.

Every time I saw Sharon the infatuation grew. I wasn't too careful about entertaining thoughts, as I believed it was an impossible relationship. I could feed my romantic glands with no danger of consummation. It was becoming obsessive though and this was starting to worry me. I was a little alarmed at how I could feel this way toward a woman but I was convinced that it was all simply in my mind. Nothing could come of it.

During these months of confusion I visited Wellington and one of my friends, a young man, told me that a very well-known pastor had interfered with him sexually when he was younger. It was so unbelievable that this much-respected man of God could do this, but the evidence my friend presented was beyond question. He had talked to others who had also encountered the advances of this pastor. This added to my confusion as I was now fighting my own passions for same-sex love. If this man, who seemed so gifted by God, did not have power over his own tendencies, what hope did I have?

The college year ended and I graduated. This was a miracle as the year had been hard and our student body had been an unusual group. Many of us were unique characters and a third of the students had dropped out over the year. Peter Morrow had been perplexed about the personalities that had gathered in this year: "The least studious bunch I have ever seen." We had wonderful input with a great Bible teacher, Ern

Baxter, living with us for a number of months. It was a pressure-cooker year and in my final night I took off the lid.

At Sharon's that night I had not contemplated that I would have to share her bed. A thrill of fear and of anticipation gripped me. Her flatmate was with us too but this only meant we couldn't talk. Up until now I had secret enjoyment as sometimes the pastor would ask everyone in the service to take the hand of the people next to them to link across the room. All the hours and nights we had talked, and now I was in her bed.

In my mind Sharon had never given me any indication of having the feelings that I had. Yet she was a very affectionate person and thought nothing of giving me hugs, and now she had curled about me, I thought, like an innocent, loving sister.

She lay with her arm behind my head, linking her fingers with mine. She was awake. I was sure she could hear my heart thumping. I was excruciatingly uncomfortable. To try to cover my heartbeat, I turned over, but now I was almost face to face with her.

For what seemed to be hours, we lay like this, face to face. Our faces drew closer and closer until our lips nearly touched. I was nearly out of my mind. I could stand it no longer and kissed her. Her eyes widened and she looked at me with shock for a moment, then she responded. In the silence we said nothing but now the act was started, on this my graduation night, there was no going back.

In the morning Sharon's flatmate went to work. We breathed at last and Sharon said, "What happened? Why did you do that!"

I was dumbfounded. She had hardly been a blameless party. We talked. It just couldn't happen. We both agreed. It was illicit. It was sin. It was forbidden and unthinkable. We were Pentecostal Christians. I had just graduated from college. What were we thinking? It was a bit of a relief. We both confessed that this had been very wrong. It could not go on.

The next two nights were worse. The illicit factor only heightened the attraction. I was more in love with this girl than I had ever been with anyone in all my years of relationships. Nothing had met this total absorption. I felt as if we were merged as one person. I couldn't live without her. She was quick to respond and initiate and neither of us was able to stop what had now begun like a bush fire.

But I couldn't live without God either. Where was he?

I flew home and in the days that followed, I wanted to hide from what I knew was a holy God. I spent hours and hours in the hot sun digging up our back garden, pulling weeds, hiding in the garden like Adam.[5] I was afraid. Afraid that this holy God would send a lightning bolt, or at least a fatal car accident, to punish me.

My isolation from God and the loneliness in my parents' home saw me writing to Sharon, ringing Sharon, desperate to see her again. Nothing had consumed me more fully. Even how I had felt about Greg was not like this. With the feelings I had for him, I retained some sort of sanity.

We planned for Sharon to come and visit Auckland. I counted the days until she came. My mother saw our likeness and could barely tell us apart. I revelled in this. My father remarked to my sister that he thought that my friend and I had a relationship that bordered on lesbianism. My sister, who knew all my struggles, said nothing but warned me to be more discreet. She was not happy but wanted to help me through this, and knowing the way that my parents would react, it would have been far from pleasant if they had learned the truth.

The term "lesbian" never came into it as far as I was concerned. If anyone had asked if I was lesbian I would have said, "No". I was not homosexual; I just loved Sharon. We were soul mates. I had found my other half and it was not my fault that one of us was wrongly trapped in a female body!

Discretion was far from my mind. God was pushed to the side. I couldn't understand what He wanted of me. I did still want to please Him but He was so silent. He had never provided me with love like this. He had sent me with false hope into the jaws of shame at that church now far behind me. Sharon went home and I now planned to visit her.

Sharon's flatmate had realized what had happened and was very upset. Sharon had moved in with someone new. This new flatmate was a friend of mine. Sharon told me that she had confided in her new flatmate, Ella, who was determined to help Sharon to overcome this sin. Ella had been disgusted with me, having been a friend of mine. She was so disgusted that she had felt the need to tell all the church pastors and many of my student colleagues.

Sharon thought it best if I came down to see her while Ella was away on a holiday for two weeks. I couldn't wait to see Sharon. Whatever she said was OK with me.

When I arrived Sharon made it very clear to me that she wanted no physical relationship. She was determined to go on for God. I had to accept this. I admired her strength. I had thought of nothing but Sharon the whole time we had been apart. I wouldn't force the issue, I was just glad to be with her, in her company. Any idol of mine could do with me as they liked.

It was only a matter of days before we resumed where we had left off. Now since we had more time to talk and consider where this was going, the guilt began to set in. Toward the end of the stay we decided that we had better go to a counsellor at the church to get our lives straightened out. I had already been to the counsellor before I had left college to tell him I was struggling with thoughts about homosexuality. He had given me the answer "Just look to Jesus." I tried to, but there were conflicting photos. How did I "look to Jesus"? This had just not been enough. But I knew like a good Christian girl that it should be enough.

We went back to this man. Both of us confessed our sin and he prayed for us, but also told the only uncle that I had. I had loved this uncle, as he was one of the few people in my childhood who seemed to genuinely love me for me. I wondered as the subsequent years went by why my uncle was so uncomfortable around me. Why he now only recognized my sister's birthday and I seemed to become a "non-person". He was a wonderful, godly man but I think that this knowledge stretched his grace a little too far. I learned of his knowledge many years later.

I wished then that I could have explained to him so many factors that, while not excusing my actions and behaviour, had certainly contributed to them. One was the sexual interference of a trusted elderly man, who with his wife, babysat me when I was between six and seven years of age, every Friday night. How would my parents ever have known what took place when the wife was busy somewhere else? The elderly couple were good church-going people.

How could I have explained to my uncle the relationship breakdowns in our outwardly healthy-looking family? The demanding, compulsive love that my mother wanted from me but was so unable to give in return. The distant and damaged father who couldn't remember my name and called me a derivative of my name and my sister's, Sh'Evelyn. The father who once patted me on the head when I was ten, so that I cherished this one moment of affection throughout my entire childhood.

The way my mother had used to pull me into line as a child was by threatening me with her death. "If you do that you will kill me!"

"Your mother is a sick woman. She could die any time," my father would confirm.

"I have a weak heart. One of these days you will find me dead and it will be your fault."

And the other observation I often heard was "You're just like your brother. One day they will come to take you away."

More especially, the constant imminent death of my mother became too much of a strain for me as a young girl. So one night, as I lay in bed, I mustered my graphic imagination, and lived through the day of my mother's death. I saw her die and lie there, cold. I wept and wept and said my goodbyes. Then I went to sleep. She couldn't hurt me any more. She was already dead. Every time I heard the threat, I remembered she was already dead. She went on toppling fragilely on the verge of death to the ripe old age of 84.

As I grew into later adulthood I could see the shortcomings, but I could see also where they began, and seeing my parents' own pain and the lives they had survived as children, I was able to forgive them. Up until I saw this, I felt nothing but pity or repulsion for my parents. Until I was in my mid-twenties, I blamed them for everything.

More than everything being my parents' fault, they owed me. From the age of sixteen they had never had to pay another cent for me. I was told in one argument that I owed them for my upbringing. I made sure that in one way or another I paid them back financially. I would not be in debt to them. But I resented this. I resented that they could have paid for me to return to school to have a better education. I resented that I had to educate myself. I resented that I had to live on what were at that time meagre female wages, shifting from one scummy flat to the next.

I came home. I had to try to get back to the Lord. I knew that realistically I had to work through this newly awakened desire. It was not right in God's sight and never could be. I could try and twist the scriptures to get them to say what I wanted, but this would not change essential truth.

My old friend, Rachael, took a flat with me and we agreed to try to get me back on track. I would go back to the Baptist church I had been in and find out what it was that God wanted me to do, now that I had finished Bible College. I would try to find a nice Christian man and I would marry him and get over all this. There were prospects; Greg wasn't the only fish in the sea, although I still saw no equal and now had no real interest in males.

For a year I persevered at the Baptist church. I lived for every letter from Sharon, though they were platonic. She seemed to be doing so well. About three-quarters of the way through this year she wrote to tell me that Greg had just got engaged. This was now nearly a year since the pastor's daughter had told me he was already engaged. Sharon had heard this news through the pastor's daughter, who she now explained had always had an interest in Greg.

At least the pastor's daughter was not the one to marry him. But I had never felt so betrayed.

Chapter 7

It was as if I had been transported back to the days before I turned sixteen. The young men in the church were slow to take any notice. How was I going to overcome this emptiness now? For years I had put my hope in Greg. Sharon had stolen my pent-up adoration and now a relationship with her was illegal. Surely God would give me a good husband and I could walk away from the failings of my past. Days dragged on and to fill my void, I began to toy with other ways to enjoy life. My foot in both worlds set me on the fringe of church life. I was more comfortable here.

A new group of friends were just as happy to go to a city pub for a few drinks on a Saturday night, or a party with drink, before waking to a solid Bible service at the church on Sunday. Sometimes a hangover might keep me from the service, but I wasn't going to be straitjacketed. A girl had to have a life! Feelings meant everything to me. If I felt bad, then the mandate was to change this and feel good and good feelings were always right.

Toward the end of this year I was starting to think I had life a little more in order. My friend Rachael and I would go out for meals or to a pub and to feel like this was freedom. We were grown up enough to do this and to hold on to our faith at the same time. I began to think I could work through the strange episode with Sharon. It had all been a bit of a mistake.

Then Sharon told me that she and Ella were coming to live in Auckland. She wanted to see me. Now that I was months from our affair, I was a bit wary. I had never totally lost my feelings for Sharon and had made no secret of this to her. She was adamant that there was to be nothing in our meeting. She just wanted to talk. She didn't want Ella there.

We met in a café. Her voice: I had forgotten what a pleasant voice she had and the way she spoke. There was nothing vulnerable about Sharon. I needed her strength. Ella, she explained, was very possessive in her friendship. I accepted this could be so. It was terrible living with Ella, she explained. She had no freedom and she felt suffocated.

"Are you 'with' Ella?" I tested.

"Don't be ridiculous!" Sharon countered. "I just can't live with her dominating me. Can you help me?"

Help Sharon? Was she crazy? I would have rushed around right now to move her out. Anything!

"No, no. You can't do anything too radical. You have to help me think about how to get away."

We met again several times. Gradually a story of a close possessive friendship came out. Then stories of Ella hitting Sharon. What was this? Flatmates didn't hit each other. Was she sure that they weren't in a relationship? No, I was just suspicious. Besides, now that we were meeting again, Sharon realized that she wanted to be with me. I was delirious. Nothing could have made me happier.

We decided that we would get away for a weekend and go to a motel. This way we could talk and plan what should be done. Logic and good intention was over. This was it. I couldn't live without Sharon. I had heard nothing from God for over a year. The heavens were in silence, no visions, no dreams, and no special scriptures. I simply had heard nothing from God from the day I believed he had directed me to a certain church in Christchurch.

Sharon found some way to get away from Ella. We met at our clandestine motel. One of us had supplied the wine. I don't remember who. There was nothing to hold back my devouring craving for Sharon.

Nothing she could say or do would break the love I now found was absolute. Not even the disclosure that, yes, after all, she and Ella had been in a relationship all year. Pretty much from the start. Even when Ella was busy disparaging me to all the church leaders. No one had known, but now Sharon was sorry and could see that I was the only one she had ever wanted to be with.

One weekend wasn't enough. I wasn't ready to just walk away from all my friends and with the situation with Ella there was no way we could simply start a life together. It would have been impossible in Auckland under the eyes of my parents, or in Wellington under the eyes of hers. The only other city I knew was Christchurch. Impossible.

We planned a week in Coromandel to think about what we should do. This rugged coastal area was peaceful and beautiful. There were cheap cabins we could stay in and no one could trace us there.

I had never been so happy. I told Rachael and she was sad that I had gone this way but she was busy trying to put her own life together. She thought I was foolish and wasn't sure that she trusted Sharon, but who was she to make my decisions? She would still be my friend.

Rachael had been moving through similar questioning of her faith and what life meant to her. She had a boyfriend now, who I didn't like. We had met him at a bar in town. He and I were mutual in our distaste for each other and neither tried to hide it. By this time we were flatting in Rachael's parents' home while they were overseas. Her brother Paul had moved in as well, and he was as much a brother to me as I had ever had. We had practically all grown up together. I had spent so much time staying in their home from the age of twelve that their home was a second home to me.

I wrote later in my diary how I felt travelling to Coromandel. Nothing of the scenery mattered, the farmland, the craggy seascapes. Sharon was my happiness. I wrote of her eyes, that they were so blue that I wanted to swim in them. When I was about ten I used to lie on a summer day on the newly cut, long grass on the paddock near our school. I could smell the good, wholesome stalks of drying grasses. I would look up into an azure sky and feel myself wanting to dive upward to swim in the blueness of the sky. I couldn't unite with the sky but the sky had come to me in Sharon.

We had such a great week. Sharon made me do risky things that I would never have done on my own. Hitching rides with a local cream delivery man to see the end of the peninsular on a cold misty morning. We stopped in the dark in a desolate place, for him to show us the glow-worms shining clear in the early morning cold. Playing darts at the Golconda Hotel and winning a crate of beer. Getting drunk with the locals and listening to Suzie Quatro on an old jukebox. Visiting the local oyster farm and sitting on a wharf eating the oysters straight from the shell. We talked locals into taking us everywhere. Sharon seemed to have little fear of anyone.

If I couldn't have God and Sharon, then it had to be Sharon. God had never made me feel like this. If I were worshipping Sharon, perhaps I would be killed in a moment of God's anger. I had to risk this. It wasn't my fault that I was confused. There was no way I could go back to Christchurch and follow his direction for me now. We were making plans to create a new life. We would go back to our homes and save as fast as we could. I would stay in Auckland in my flatting situation and she would go home to her mother. We would buy tickets and go to live in Australia where no one knew us. Unbelievable bliss was a few months away at the most. I still didn't see myself as lesbian.

If God was love and this was undoubtedly the most intense love I had ever known, then God must somehow accept what was happening. Deep in my heart I knew this to be ridiculous but since other Christians that we confided in told us that this was the case, then it could be true. Love like this couldn't be wrong.

Sharon left and I was OK for a time. I could write and phone. We had seen as much of each other as we could before she left. My path was set. I lived again for her every letter or call. Then something began to feel wrong. I didn't know why but Sharon was sounding strange.

I started to feel a knot of insecurity. What was happening down there in Wellington?

"Don't worry, everything is OK," she comforted.

"I want to come down."

"No! Don't do that. Not yet anyway. Don't come unless I say you can."

"What's going on?"

"Nothing! Just calm down."

I was caged. The feeling increased. I had to go to Wellington to see what was going on. I had to be reassured.

The all-day trip on the train was torment, minute by minute, hour by hour. Sharon knew I was on my way. The young girl of thirteen seated next to me flirted with me all the way down. All I wanted to do was keep a can of beer in front of me to dull the growing ache.

As the girl got off the train at her town just before Wellington, she said, "Well, are you going to kiss me?"

"What!" I was bewildered at what I was hearing. I had said nothing of my life to this girl.

"Forget it!" she said in a huff, as she pulled her bags down to leave the train. I looked at this girl with perplexity. Was I wearing a badge that said, "Pick me. I am a lesbian"?

I arrived and went to find Sharon. After going to her parents' house and finding everyone had gone to work, I phoned later and was told that Sharon had been staying with a "friend".

I had to track her down and went to see the friend whom I had met once before. Sharon had wanted me to meet Anne since she been a lesbian for years, living with a long-term girlfriend. I knew where she worked and figured that she might know where Sharon was. She did. Sharon was with this girl's own lover. She had moved in and now Anne was heartbroken.

I died on the spot, my first death. All my premonitions were right. The intensity of love turned almost overnight to a deep hatred. I had given up everything for Sharon! My heart was in fragments. I lost my voice. Shock turned into flu. The depression was as deep as the euphoria had been. Only now I knew I had no God to turn to either.

In anger and hurt, I fell into step with Anne. Within days a new relationship had begun. I just moved my craving for love over to Anne. Now a new plan was plotted. Anne would come to live with me in Auckland. I would go home and get a flat for us. There was some comfort in this. I had found work at her office for a few weeks and we had spent some time together by the time I headed back north.

I found a flat on the edge of the suburb of Newmarket and a few weeks later Anne arrived. I hadn't known her very long but already I could see something was wrong. She was remote. In Wellington it had all seemed simple. We would try to make a go of it. I was no longer alone again. Anne had long golden hair and a warm personality. Again she seemed so much more capable of handling life than I was. Sharon and Anne were both competent in their jobs, working in offices. I still felt inferior to most people.

Anne had been in the Wellington gay scene for a long time and had friends in Auckland. She knew where the girls' club was and where the girls drank. We went out. I was shy and unaccustomed to this lifestyle and not sure that this was how I wanted to live. I just wanted a soulmate. Was that too much to ask?

Anne lasted about two months. I had lucked out with perfect timing. In the two weeks before Anne had left Wellington, she had been to a party and met the real "love of her life". Now she couldn't live without this wonderful American woman.

"Sorry, Shirley, I hadn't planned it this way, but I have to go."

Sitting in my flat drinking tequila with my guitar and singing sad songs that I wrote, I was now dragged into a pit of self-pity and wallowing misery. I clung to the curves of the guitar like a surrogate lover and the bottle was starting to become a more faithful friend than anyone I had yet met.

I tried to consider getting my life together. I tried to go back to church and to God. But already I was hooked. I couldn't go back. This new drug of female lovers was too intoxicating. No man had made me feel like this. A woman after all, I reasoned, would have to know how to please another woman more than a man would. Women understood women, only another woman was going to satisfy my longing for love. My soulmate had to be out there. One who didn't lie, one looking for true love, like me.

I went back to Rachael's. By now it was just her brother and I and his friend flatting there. Rachael was teaching at a school in the country. Being in what was now a suburban, "straight" lifestyle again, I started to wither in my loneliness. Paul and I would go out and both eye girls as we cruised Queen Street. I loved his company and he accepted me like a male chum. He wanted a girlfriend and so did I. His chances were better than mine were. I didn't have any connections in the gay world. I had only been to the club once with Anne and I certainly wasn't going to go there on my own.

This was the time that I started to drink spirits. The hot fire of whisky or rum burning down my throat dulled my sorrow. I went back for more punishment from the bottle and because I had grown up in a home where wine was only ever drunk as one glass on Christmas day, or sherry for "medicinal purposes", I had no sense. The more I could pour down before I was ill or fell asleep, the better.

The worst part of my drinking binges all through these years was that unlike other alcoholic friends, I never blacked out and I always remembered what I had done the night before.

Rachael married her boyfriend. I was so self-consumed and unaquainted with the rituals of life that I did nothing to help. I was the bridesmaid but, apart from turning up almost a zombie on Valium in order to get up the aisle with all those eyes looking at me, I was useless. My sister had married as well, the week I returned from my fateful visit to Sharon. I was her bridesmaid too. The nervousness I felt on these days was so dreadful that I was glad I was far from ever being a bride myself. I would have nightmares of being a bride. All those eyes looking at me.

I knew that there was a little bar where gay men drank and sometimes the girls would go there. It was my only hope. I would go to the bar after my night-classes. I was now studying NZ Certificate in Management. I was the only girl in two classes but this was my area of interest, developing people and organizing. I had been told not to expect much prospect of a job after I qualified. Men held most management positions. I would be better to stick with typing.

The options open to girls when I left school were office work, teaching, shop work or nursing. I didn't want to do any of these things. I had wanted to go to university but my parents had decided that if I wanted to go back to school I would have to find some way to pay for myself. At school, I was in a graded system and in the top class, but the rot had set in. My social life and the seeds of malfunction from my upbringing had begun to flower into all the wayward behaviour that was not compatible with going back to school anyway.

What was the use? I was interested in psychology, English

and physics. Where would that get me? My parents' expectation was that a girl would marry anyway and why should she need a career? Once the ring was on the finger, she never needed to work again. I half believed this, but in my new lifestyle, I doubted the ring would present itself. I was going to have to fend for myself.

I had to try to get my earning power up; women's wages in most jobs were about half the equivalent man's wage, for the same job. I had to try to get into something more satisfying and something that might pay better.

Actually the satisfaction was more important to me than the money. My hippie roots had taught me to scorn money. The gurus of this movement meanwhile had moved on to maturity and were busy creating new companies and forming stronger capitalistic views than even their parents had held. I should have known their preaching was idealistic from the start.

What about that Christmas when we were urged to consider the starving of the world? We would all fast on Christmas Day to protest the indulgence of the bourgeoisie. We'd meet in the band rotunda at Albert Park. On the actual day, there was my sister, one other disillusioned young man and myself. Our beloved leaders were no doubt scraping the last forks of meat and gravy up to their greased lips, their eyes gleaming as they saw the pot boiling in the kitchen with mum's famous Christmas pud.

Idealism, when believed by zealots like me, died slowly. I only needed enough to pay my rent, my bus fares and my necessary grog. However, one day I wanted my own home. No man was going to provide this. If I was going to have to work all my life, I didn't want to be slaving at some factory assembly line.

When I came back from Bible College I knew that I had to do something about a career. I really wasn't qualified at anything. I didn't want to work in bookshops or cafés all my life.

With the way things were going with Sharon, I would never marry. I had tried all sorts: radio factories, bakeries, shop work, basic office work. Everything so far had been boring. I had to get some qualifications to lift myself above these unskilled jobs.

In my first year back from Bible College, while I flatted with Rachael, I went to a secretarial college, finally seeing that I had to have some sort of saleable skill. I worked by night cleaning an office building to pay my way, but Rachael made up the shortfall. This got me into secretarial work. I worked as a shorthand typist, although I had never taken shorthand as a subject. While I had been in Bible College, I had invented a form of speed writing to get my notes down. I never found a boss who could dictate faster than I could get down his notes, so they never knew the difference.

I hated secretarial work. I would look on and think, "I could run this place." I especially disliked much of the lack of skill I saw in the management of people. Why shouldn't I consider running some business myself? But I would need more education. No woman would even be considered to manage a shoe shop unless she owned it or had double the degrees of any male in the field.

I would start somewhere. So I began to take papers in management and had a supervision certificate at the time I found a career that took my interest. By the time Anne had left me, I had started working for an inbound tour company. At last this was work that had pressure and challenge. I could learn in this job and much of the job was researching. I loved the position in the "special interest" area where I could combine my love of organizing with working in a team.

I was given all the horse buyers' tours, since I had taken a new interest in horse racing. At one time I could have told anyone where the best horse studs were and which horses sired by what stallion were up for sale. I never won after the

first time I went to the races and won $13, but I went reli-
giously. It was my new church. I went on my own and drank
between races. In Sydney I would discover the joys of one-
armed bandits and the roulette table.

New Zealand then had only the races. One time I met a
young Indian man and we went out for a meal. He was very
concerned about me. I gave him the ring Sharon had given me.
He had treated me with respect and kindness. I wanted to give
him a gift, but it was an act of disparagement, a final insult to
my fallen god, to give the ring to a perfect stranger.

Chapter 8

There was no longer any pretence of trying to follow Jesus. I still knew him to be the truth. I had seen too much to not believe, but I just couldn't live the life. I could never blaspheme. No matter how bad my language became and how drunk or out of it I was, I could not blaspheme the name of God. I was keenly aware of my state.

My laughter, I had noticed, had gone hollow. I could almost have drawn a graph of my joy draining from me. I hadn't known that I had joy until I lost it. To me there was no way I could believe that I could be both homosexual and righteous before God. I knew when I was in relationship with him and he was with me, and I was very conscious now that he was not there. Anyone who tried to convince me that it was possible to be both, I knew could never have sensed his presence or known him personally, or they couldn't have made this claim.

I continued to drink at a tiny, underground bar. Sometimes girls would come in and I began to recognize some of them. I was too nervous to go and meet them. They looked intimidating. I did get to know some of the guys. One was a brother of a schoolboy I had known. They invited me to a few parties.

There was one girl who was, like me, a loner on the outside. I started to befriend her and together we decided to visit the club. The isolation from my own kind was driving me to seek out where I belonged.

The club was a large room above a motorbike shop near the central railway station. To get there, we would ascend a narrow staircase and enter to see a rough wooden bar. The floor was sticky with beer even when it was washed. There was a small patch of carpet, black with spilt drinks that stuck to the shoes as you walked over it. A few small tables with chairs were in this area. If anyone looked in daylight into the tins that stored the potato chips, they were likely to find a dead mouse or two.

By one wall was a jukebox with a selection of dance music. Disco and romantic ballads were sovereign. The floor was bare for dancing and the odd fight. Next to the other wall was the "holy" pool table and in the far corner a small built-in toilet. In later years, behind the "holy" pool table was a mural that I had painted. It was a landscape but the hills were the forms of naked women.

It was illegal for the club to sell liquor but this was no problem. It was casually called a sport's club with a vague connection to a girls' softball team. This meant it could sell drink cards. Buy a card and you were entitled to ten drinks. No problem, just keep selling cards all night and the drink could keep flowing. Bring your own smoking selection. No males were permitted, although the occasional transvestite would come.

In these initial days, with my new friend, we could arrive with a few drinks under the belt and take in the surroundings together. I began to meet more people. Life was looking up. At home, Paul's friend was annoyed to find out I was lesbian and thought I might go for his girlfriend, so he punched me. I thought this was hilarious. Little did he know I had vowed to never convert any "straight" girl. I took it as a compliment that he saw me as competition!

This was the only time I ever met hostility toward my new lifestyle. Sometimes at work I would see people talking behind their hands with disparaging remarks and I knew I was the subject. Yet often the same people would be vying to be known by me or, worse if they were women, would try for my attention.

I had found a new level of popularity that was never accorded me as a Christian. As a Christian in the workplace, I was always made to feel an outcast. This was far less acceptable and more despicable than being gay. No one wanted to know about my life as a Christian or why I believed what I did. Many were fascinated with why I had a sexual preference for women.

Some of the girls I had seen in the bar now became my friends. I was in! I felt more at home than I had ever felt in the church. I belonged here. Drink meant that I didn't have to be caught in my inhibitions. I could let the real me out. I imagined that at last I would be able to sing solo, speak to crowds and take control of my life. I did sing solo at pubs with anything but skill. I did speak but it was only to scream abuse at anyone unfortunate enough to cross me when I was high on spirits.

There was a sort of honour among us though. Whatever I did one week that might be despicable would be trumped by someone before too long. Things were forgotten and forgiven quickly. Not like in the church. We were all one society. There was little to have to live up to.

It was confusing. Was it that I was a man trapped in a woman's short, big-busted body? Should I consider a sex change? I would make a very short male. Any woman in the scene attracted me. I wasn't too fussy. They didn't have to be good-looking, nor have a mind. The only criterion was that moment of magnetic eye contact and something I could latch onto that made them superior to me.

I found another girlfriend, a diminutive girl with raven hair. It was complicated and her last relationship had never quite ended. It wasn't worth it and besides I liked her ex-girlfriend too much as a friend too. I met another young girl, very pretty with long dark hair and girlish freckles. She was a body builder and very young. It was no meeting of the minds, but she amused me. I thought I had fallen in love again and she moved in. She was 17, the product of an abused background. Life for her had to be on a surface level only, because it had already been too hard. Abuse from an uncle from the age of three had sealed her fate.

Soon she found someone else and the rage I had built up from so much accumulated hurt surfaced through this break-up. One night I was in a bush suburb where she was meeting this new girlfriend. We had been drinking at someone's house. I had been left while they went to get more drink. The neighbours were treated to a barrage of filthy, abusive language. The world deserved my spleen.

Depression set in and in the early hours of the morning I phoned my headmaster from my primary school days. He had been one person who had believed in me as a child and now I couldn't think of anyone else to call. He was surprised and did remember me. I had been a very special student to him as he had nurtured what he saw as an immature gift to write. He was gracious but I could remember little of the conversation. Years later as I remembered this foolish night, I phoned and apologized to him.

My now ex-girlfriend returned and I met her on the driveway. I was on my way with her new friend's car keys to drive her car over the bank in revenge. For this I was punched flat to the ground. I noted as I floated backwards that there was no pain. Blessed drink!

Another relationship followed. Again I picked up with the aggrieved partner. For a few short months I lived with Lexie. She had been a sports star at my old high school. I was impressed with this solid, blonde woman. I had never been good at sport and hated anything to do with it so much that I would choose to write essays in the library, rather than go on a cross country run.

She was very physical and we would fight. She was bigger than I was and I always lost. The relationship was the closest

I came to living with a wife-beater. Lexie would go out with her team-mates drinking. I was expected to stay home in the flat we had moved into and have dinner ready, at whatever time she came home. I wasn't to go out and my new friends became my drinking neighbours.

A few times I tracked Lexie down and made scenes at her sports socials. I would get a hiding for this and feel grateful that she had paid me attention. In sober mornings I would blame myself and try to please her more. She was taking out other girls but I should learn to live with this. The more she beat me, the more I clung to her.

One time in a jealous rage I had bitten her shoulder; she probably still bears the tattoo. Another time, I had aggravated her and with one quick punch from her softball-batting arm, she had broken my nose. Explaining days off sick due to the grog was one thing, but going to the office with two black eyes and a swollen nose was difficult. Work life was reasonably normal but my life outside of work was a jungle. I was quite proud of the small ding in my nose. My war scar. I owed Lexie though and I would bide my time. I never forgot an offence like this. Sharon's fate would be horrible too. I owed her more pain than I owed any other.

Twice during this time I drank until I saw snakes or fire filling the room. I would be unable to walk. I once found myself in an inner city apartment with a group of drunks I barely knew. I was trapped, unable to move on a mattress on the floor, seeing snakes writhing all around me, but I couldn't kill them or get away from them. The crate of beer, the bottle of whisky, the wine, was destroying me. My life was in danger but I was sprawled across the path to the fridge.

"She deserves it, trash!" a voice said.

"Get me another beer!" someone else shouted as they kicked me in passing.

In the morning, I crawled out of the house and skulked

home. I hoped that the binge had killed off some of my brain cells so that I could stop thinking. I had a vague idea this time of how close I had come to death. That was the day I gave up spirits. Beer and wine were safer.

One of my friends was working at a pub across town. I went over sometimes just for company and to play pool. One Saturday I met the owner of the hotel, a man in his forties; he owned property around the country. I also met some of the other patrons and one young man asked me out.

At this stage I felt as if I had seen enough of this gay life. I could go no lower and wondered if maybe I could just be interested in a male. Was it possible that I had forgotten heterosexual sex? Perhaps I should try. I accepted his invitation clinically. I barely took a look at him.

We went out one Friday night. I just wanted to get on with it and drank myself to a dull complacency. I went home with him and slept with him. It was horrible. He was so happy and showed me the photos of his children by his ex-wife. He had big ears. They had big ears; I hoped I wasn't pregnant. I felt sorry for him; he was a nice guy but my experiment had been tried and had failed. I was a confirmed lesbian.

I went home and considered this realization. No men for me ever again. I had done with this crazy notion that I could fit back into society's majority. Lexie had gone somewhere for the weekend so I was contemplating a lonely Saturday night. My barmaid friend called and said that the owner of the pub wanted me to come over. He had heard that I worked in inbound tourism and wanted to talk to me about this.

I had been sipping sherry from a cheap flagon half the afternoon so I took the offer of a free taxi to enjoy some company for the evening. The owner plied me with my favourite drink, brandy Alexander.

"Come with me, I want to show you something," he said early in the night. I stupidly followed him and as I stumbled in my intoxication, realized too late that I was being led upstairs to his flat. I tried to fight him but he was stronger and he bruised my arms as he dragged me upstairs.

There was no point fighting him. I was too drunk. I was sick. He didn't care. All night he raped and abused me and, despite the drink, I was conscious of my own witlessness in falling into this trap from the start.

In the morning he sent me home in a taxi. I spent all morning in the bath scrubbing myself and feeling sick. I couldn't blame him. I had a new badge now that said, "Abuse me." It was what I deserved. Certainly I wouldn't bother reporting him to the police; who would believe or care what happened to a dyke? Others had singled me out for abuse at work parties, but this had been the worst.

This hotel owner haunted me for a little while. He had the cheek to turn up at my workplace and ask me if I would be his mistress. I told him I would have been more interested in the beautiful wife I heard he had. She didn't deserve him. I was astounded at his audacity coming to see me. He met with me again a month or so later when I was on a coach tour, experiencing the company's Northland product.

He knew I was on the tour and came to repeat his entrapment with drink. I accepted the offer of wine, choosing the most expensive bottle of champagne the hotel had on offer, and then befriended a gay man working at the hotel, confided in him and got him to take me home. My gay friend was grateful as it served his purpose too. He was under suspicion and wanted to keep his own preferences to himself. This would take the heat off him for some time too. I had some satisfaction out of it all, seeing the hotel owner's face as we left.

Perhaps I had been born to be worthless but even so, why did I have to put up with Lexie any more? Why should I keep any ethics and remain faithful? There had to be other girls out there whom I could love, who wouldn't hit me. I had an affair.

Lexie found out and there was a horrible showdown at the club. I saw the full bottle flying through the air and ducked just in time. My new lover collected it behind me. I enjoyed this brawl. At last Lexie was getting a fight with an equal. As she left, I took my opportunity and put my stiletto heel into her stomach, sending her backwards down the stairs from the top to the street.

By now, I was one of three running the club. I bought in all the booze, and Millie and I placated the odd detectives that came for a look.

"Millie," I asked in the early days, "why is the club called the KG Club?"

"That's easy," she explained. "It was started years ago by two girls who rented a small place in Karangahape Road. KG; Karangahape Girls' Club."

"But we're not in K' Road now."

"Yeah, but everyone knew it as KG; they've all forgotten why it was called that anyway. I don't even remember who the original girls were now."

"Pity. The history needs to be written."

Millie looked at me quizzically with her large brown eyes. I was a strange bird, thinking too much all the time. What did it matter?

Millie was big and had a wonderful innocence and an infectious, merry laugh that endeared her to the police. I could talk and think my way through situations. They knew us, knew about the illegal dealings, had no doubt of the blue haze in the room, but we amused them and did little real harm. As long as we kept to ourselves in the rat-hole above the bike shop, we were contained.

"How's it going tonight, Shirley?"

"Fine, fine. No trouble." We looked after our own skirmishes. A primitive law existed.

I started to enjoy brawls; they made for a good night at

the pub. The girls all drank at one small inner city pub and I knew the right place to be, by a low window, so that I could incite a stool-throwing, fist-flying battle, before slipping out the window. Fighting wasn't for me. I couldn't win. Not even watching episodes on TV of *On the Mat – Professional Wrestling*, gave me any better skill.

I wallowed in being a "low-life": going to a lovely family picnic site at a beach where our group would proceed to swim half naked, scavenging shellfish, eating them raw and drinking from cans. We'd get louder and more obnoxious and thought nothing of flaunting our behaviour. Family groups would move quietly away with looks of contempt and disgust. Who cared? I belonged.

We partied and the only prerequisite was plenty of beer. Some said I had missed my calling; I should have been a paid stripper! But then I would have had to perform for men and that to me, even for money, was abhorrent.

Free again from a relationship, the club was my life. There didn't seem any good prospects so Millie and I spent more time just drinking and partying with friends. I was now 23, still young; there was still hope for love.

One night a young girl, lean and attractive, came in. She was with an older woman but they didn't seem to be together. I asked the young girl to dance. She could dance and that was a good start. Right away, I was back in a relationship but Monica had a problem. She couldn't move in with me.

The older woman was from the Justice Department. She had wanted Monica to blend with her own kind to assimilate back into a normal life, and had brought her to the club. Monica was under the courts on periodic detention. Her circumstances were unusual.

In the first few weeks that Monica stayed with me, on one night, I woke with a start and saw a large, plain-faced girl standing over her with a knife poised to strike. I shrieked and rose up to fend her off with my arm, and the spectre disappeared. It had been a clear apparition or vision. I described the girl and Monica shrugged. "That's Nita; she's into all that stuff, astral projection. She hates me right now because I am with you." I had yet to learn about Nita.

Monica's mother had remarried. The new husband had children by the first wife and one was a girl, Nita, a few years younger than Monica. They had ended up in a relationship. The problem for Monica was that she was sixteen when it began and her stepsister was thirteen. Neither had been innocent before this, but Nita's young age meant trouble. By the time Monica was 18, Nita had been sent to a boarding school to break up the relationship. Letters were sent pleading for Monica to visit. Monica had been warned that if she made any attempt to see Nita she would be arrested.

The letters kept coming and Nita wanted Monica to bring money. Monica decided to take the risk: she would go down and meet Nita outside her school. She took the long drive and waited. As soon as Nita joined her in the car, there was a detective right there. Monica was taken to Mt Eden prison and kept there on remand. She was charged with carnal knowledge, basically numerous counts of rape or sex with a minor.

To avoid Nita having to go to court to testify, Monica pleaded guilty. She was sentenced to 18 months probation and six months periodic detention. She spent several months in Mt Eden prison on remand. When I met her she was still on probation. One of the conditions of this probation was that she had to live with a legal guardian, who at that time was her mother. In order for Monica to move in with me, I had to become her legal guardian.

The women at the courts were very sympathetic. It was a unique situation and most felt that Monica had been given a more severe sentence than she deserved. The 18 months were designed to get Nita to sixteen, the legal age of consent. Monica was forbidden to see Nita up until then.

The courts signed Monica over to me and she moved in. This was the start of my longest live-in relationship.

Monica was keen for me to meet Nita and so we had an evening with the whole family. We had a few drinks and I tried to befriend Nita because I felt a bit sorry for her. In my opinion, she was a big, plain-featured, loud-mouthed girl with an unattractive personality to complete the description.

Having met Nita and having mused to myself how Monica could ever have been attracted to her, it was a horror to hear a report from Monica's probation officer.

"I had Nita and her mother in here a few days back. Nita wanted to lay a charge against you."

"What for?"

"She said that you had touched her when you visited Monica's family. She's wanting you put away for seven years."

Cold waves rolled up from my stomach and my head spun. "Touch her! I wouldn't touch that girl with a bargepole!"

"I know," said the probation officer. "Because I have come to know you, I am well aware that you would never have done this. I told Nita and her mother this, and explained that if they went ahead with the charge, I would personally go to court and stand against them!"

Soon after Monica moved in I met Jasmine, but did nothing but exchange glances. I was on the ethical up again. I would never cheat on Monica. My ability to trust and love was blunted but there was enough idealism left to believe this one could work.

Monica and I were more compatible than previous girlfriends had been. She had intelligence and personality. She lied to me often but didn't they all? Just because I was a stickler for honesty, I realized I couldn't expect this from everyone else. She flirted and had affairs, and I was livid every time, but she stayed with me. Each time, I lost a little respect and a little more trust, but we went on. She was beautiful, being of Czechoslovakian, Maori and French extraction.

She did a little modelling and had a perfectionism that meant she kept our flat immaculate. But I only ever saw her wear a dress (one of mine) once when she had to go to court. Mostly I worked and she took odd jobs now and then. All my relationships had been a bit like this. I was the breadwinner. It seemed normal to me. At least Monica could cook.

Somehow, I had managed to keep my lifestyle from my parents. I was good at scrubbing any smell of cigarettes from me before visiting. My mother insisted on my visiting every weekend, and often I must have smelled of day-after alcohol fumes but nothing had been said. It would be very hard to keep this pretence up and sooner or later, living in the same city would be dangerous. I was hardly discreet in public.

Monica and I decided to cross the Tasman and go to live in Australia, in Sydney. It was to be the first leg of a journey to the UK, but we never got further than Sydney.

Chapter 9

Flying into Sydney, I saw from my window rows and rows of
red roofs bright in the Australian sun. A surge of fresh life ran
into me. I had fallen for this city at first sight. A sense of
adventure filled me and I thought, "I will take this city." I
would make it mine. I had always hated my own home city of
Auckland, I think only because it held so much of my past and
the chains of my mother's increasing demands and domi-
nance. I was now close to 3,000 miles away.

I researched where the best areas were to rent and we
moved to the North Shore. I didn't want to live in a ghetto of
Kiwis (New Zealanders). My aim was to blend as quickly as
possible into the Australian life. I loved this city. It was fast,
sometimes brash and I saw the sun day after day. Even in winter it was dry and blue-skied. When it did rain, it deluged and
I loved this. Sydney, as we found it, was a young city with passion and fury and hope. It had its more unseemly parts and
they suited me too.

Life was great for a short time. I easily found office work
with a "temp" agency and Monica found work in a retirement
village. She loved working with old people and we were happy.
We didn't know anyone in Sydney and had to search where to
find a social life. It wasn't long before I had met some other
"girls" in our neighbourhood and they took us to the appropriate equivalent club. It wasn't as colloquial as ours had been.

Again we would ascend a stairway to an upper room. The
bar was more sophisticated and they had a licence. The dance
floor had disco lights under the square floor. It was flash! The
girls were different too, less preoccupied with finding that

one true love. Casual relationships were far more common. Sex was demystified; why complicate it with petty jealousies?

On one of our first outings, one of our new friends took us to a pub in King's Cross. We might have been more concerned if we had realized that she had picked us up in a newly converted car. We wondered why she would just park it in a back street and not even look back to lock it.

Monica and I were like naive country cousins. The room was darker and peopled with a cosmopolitan mix unheard of in the 1970s in Auckland. In the toilet, there were filthy, used syringes complete with blood. On this first night out we saw a bouncer grab a man, thump him and drag him out of a nightclub by his hair.

This was a harder life than we knew but we got used to it. I just made a mental note to not get too close to the underworld here. Our new friend had told us about a girl she knew who had ended up in Sydney harbour with concrete shoes.

"Kiwi too," she'd added, yawning slightly.

It wasn't long before Monica was back flirting and having new affairs. I was getting sick of being hurt. There wasn't much left of my hope for a stable, secure relationship. Sure, we had talked of having some sort of wedding. But even in early days it had taken me all of my cunning and strength to keep Monica from any rendezvous with her old lover, Nita, or any new one that came along. I had had enough of this dream of a life-long soulmate. The Aussies had shown me another way.

There were more places to party in Sydney, more clubs and more variety. I already had my favourite Aussie beer. Drink had no limit with me. Mostly I could stand up but sometimes I had been carried by bouncers out of a club, to be dumped swearing and cursing on a pavement. Once in Sydney my friends had managed to get me out of the gutter just long enough to stand me on my feet to catch a taxi home.

Sometimes I just stayed face down on some garage floor

until I was able to drag myself back to my flat. In Auckland I had driven miles home on motorways, seeing double. This experience mildly interested me. It is not just a comic book fabrication. It is possible to be cross-eyed drunk.

When Monica had stayed out just one night too many, I went to the flat where she was staying. The girl she had been with was bisexual and she was out on the town with some men she knew. Where her new baby was, I have no idea; she already had four who were adopted out to her sister. She was a plump, plain girl with a loud mouth and few teeth. Why Monica had bothered, I had no idea.

I found Monica in the flat in this big block of concrete cell-like units, drunk. She had collected a magnum of champagne from our flat. Her grandfather had given it to her for her twenty-first, which had been just a few weeks before. She had drunk the entire magnum.

I was furious. At least she could have left me a drink! I was looking forward to tasting this drop! I found her lying on the floor listening to a melancholy song on a record player; it was repeating over and over.

"Whad'ja doing?" I bellowed.

"I'm gonna die."

"Don't be ridiculous!" I was furious.

Monica crawled over to the corner of the room where there was a gun, possibly it was a .22, and probably it was loaded. I knew little about gun types. All I knew was that she was being utterly idiotic.

She grasped the gun. "I'm going to kill myself, yes, I am!" she drawled.

"Not while I am here you're not!" I fumed. Being sober for a change, I had more strength than she did. I grabbed the gun from her and threw her on the ground. She lay there collapsed like a deflated balloon.

"Stupid girl!" I said as I put the gun back against the wall.

So what if she got up later and picked it up? She looked like she was out cold for a while now. I wasn't going to hang around to find out. That was it. I was out for myself. No more care for anyone any longer.

When Monica came back to her senses and returned home I told her to get out. She was incensed and we had a fight. I meant it now and there was no point in going on. She had to move out.

Some of my new bisexual friends moved in to help me pay the rent. They were little help as they ate everything they could, paid nothing and expected me to help them inject heroin into their arms every time I was home. Males, females, they all came and went. I watched my new casual lover, Sue, as she introduced others to the drug. Young, healthy men would take a hit, then weeks later I would see them pale, thin, their skin sallow and their eyes dark. They struggled to keep their jobs; some ended up in prison.

One guy in the group was quite mad. I made sure that I befriended him, as he owned the gun. He boasted of being a hired hit man. He'd killed over in Western Australia; it meant nothing to him, he said. I wasn't sure whether to believe him or not, but just in case, he was my friend. We went out on the town together, to transsexual strip clubs, discos, down seedy stairs to drinking spots. I saw a lot with Len.

It was near Christmas and I was lucky if I could get a few days work. I had just enough money coming in to pay the rent and my travel costs. Not enough to buy food with. For two months odd people came and went from my flat and I starved. The cupboards were bare. Sometimes when we were out in the panel van, cruising for Sue's drug customers, we would find a flat where there was food and I would eat something. I could always go to the pub and bludge free drink from the guys. Sometimes I might get to share some chips or if I had work for a few days, there were biscuits in the office cupboards. I lost weight rapidly and this gave me a new confidence. I was lean and emotionally hardened.

A couple of times we were stopped by the police. It unnerved me that they knew not only Sue but also me by name. This was Sydney, a big city. How close was I to prison? I wanted to travel and I knew that drug offences were a big stumbling block to a clean passport. I had to consider some new friends. Sue never worried.

"You don't have to worry," she would laugh. "I get my drugs from these guys. Surplus, you know? Confiscated gear." I had never queried the abundance of dope I was supplied. As long as I had a daily free supply, why think of where it came from? I didn't know if I should believe Sue about the police. She was trying to talk me into going to Asia with her.

"You want to travel, don't you?"

"Sure, but why would a city lawyer want to buy us tickets?" What was this packet he just wanted us to bring back? This scene had not yet totally sunk in. I felt uneasy; travel or not, I didn't think I would go on this one.

Old friends moved out and a new acquaintance, a high-class call girl, moved in. It was a convenient arrangement. She had a small son and I enjoyed taking him to the zoo and Janice's lifestyle was interesting. It was a short stay and we both moved on.

One of my new friends was a blonde part-aboriginal girl who had a tattoo on her back of a woman and a snake. The picture took over her whole back. She hated Lebanese men. She had been gang raped when she was a young teen by a group of these men and had a vendetta for them. One weekend, she was "tripping" and I was just on drink. We spent the weekend searching out and taking every Lebanese man we could find for whatever we could get. Food, free drink or drugs.

I felt guilty because I had nothing against these people at all. She picked some friendly young men and gave them nothing in return. We lived off their money all weekend, going to Bondi beach to swim. We were in the clothes we had gone out in on Friday night. No matter; we swam in our knickers and topless. Family groups watched with distaste. I had lost all self-consciousness with the beer still flowing. Somehow we arrived home unscathed on Sunday afternoon in time to sleep it off before working in a respectable office the next day.

I chased infatuations, clinging to some and treating others as casual partners. A guy I knew owned a wine bar on the edge of town. He was very generous with drink for us and I would enjoy going with a woman on each arm. Now that I had no scruples and no faith in finding a life partner, I could enjoy my new status as a playgirl.

Listening to guys in pubs boasting of their conquests made me laugh. Courting and catching women had nothing to do with their masculinity or prowess as men. I could have beaten any for the count. At last I had found a way to live in this lifestyle. My own image of myself was probably far from real. But I revelled in my new skinny figure and self-assurance.

One time I went to my hairdresser for a trim. Maybe he didn't like me, or maybe the trouser suit I had worn fooled him. He cut my hair so short that it was about half an inch on top and when I put my hand through the back, no hair came through my fingers. It was a "short back and sides". At first I was horrified. I had to go back to work as a receptionist in a high-rise office with this cut. Everyone in Sydney stared at me. I couldn't hide my crimson ears.

As the week went on I grew used to this radical haircut and started to like it. About a year later, everyone was wearing short hair. When it happened to me, it must have been an experiment for the future! Not even Sydneysiders had seen a woman with hair this short before and as a bonus it added to my new image!

Finally the lease of my flat expired and I was able to let it go. I moved in with a very butch Aussie friend to save some money. She remarked that she could never contemplate a relationship with me since I was so butch. That was fine with me. This flatting situation was safer than I had been living in before and Kim was kind. Paul, Rachael's brother, had moved to Queensland and he came down one weekend to see me. We had a great time and I was thinking I might make my home in Sydney for good. With him just in the next state I had family here.

My new flat had only one drawback. My new flatmate had a transsexual friend who, now that she had been through her sex change and was virtually married, wanted to have same-sex affairs. This meant I was sometimes chased around the flat by a huge, ugly woman with three days growth on her chin. It could become a bit tiresome sometimes. Still, her straight partner was my new drug supplier so I had to tolerate it.

I experimented with new smoking material. Opium-impregnated, tripping grass, honey and mould cured, and pure hash. Some of these experiences were out-of-body nightmares. I decided to stick with the normal stuff. I would add amyl-nitrate to my repertoire since the gay guys had introduced me to this and it was readily available from chemists. It gave a short rush that heightened confidence and energy. I could dance like Fred Astaire and John Travolta rolled into one and this was paramount in the thumping pulse of a disco.

All my Auckland goods were stored at Monica's grandfather's house. He decided that he was going to sell up. I had to go back to move everything. It would be temporary. I had too many new lovers to enjoy in Sydney. I would be back as soon as I had found somewhere else to store my goods and had worked long enough to save for the return ticket.

Coming home for a visit was quite fun. Then I landed a job back in the travel industry. I started work for an outbound tour wholesaler. I could use my knowledge of organizing special interest groups but now the world was my research area. I had to learn fast: my co-worker gave me about two weeks training, then was away for months.

The job was demanding and interesting. I loved it, at least until I realized I had been employed at under the award rate. Since travel had no union it was hard to change this. Nevertheless, the experience in outbound travel was worth staying for.

I stayed with Monica's mother for a while before finding another flat. I had lived in so many flats that by now I had lived in one suburb seven times! All close to the city.

The club had moved to more acceptable premises and younger, more discerning girls were running it. It wasn't like my day. They had a proper dance floor, a proper bar and real bays with long seats and tables. They were back in K' Road.

One of the first nights I was back, I saw Jasmine. She was standing wearing her alluring perfume that nearly drove me insane. I had arrived reasonably inebriated. Arriving sober would have been unfeasible. I walked up to Jasmine and kissed her passionately, then without a word went on to spend time with my friends. There was no point in pursuit; Jasmine was in a steady relationship. Besides, in my new persona I was under the illusion that I was some sort of female Don Juan. I was never going to be pinned down again.

In my private hours in my flat alone, I hankered back to a happier time when I had known God. I wished I could get back to him. My sister said I would. She believed I had no place in the world I was now in. I doubted it was likely; I had already tried to come back a few times, without any success. Yet I recalled the prophecies I had received. How could this ever be? One thing was for sure; I knew Peter Morrow had been right about one thing: I had walked the lip of hell. It wasn't easy out here but I was learning to survive.

In some ways my lifestyle had given me some advantages.

I had at last begun to work toward a career. For one thing I had little hope of giving up work. I wouldn't marry; I wouldn't have a family. This was a big let-down. I had always wanted children. However, I wasn't about to do what some of my friends did, get pregnant to just anyone for the sake of fulfilling this.

One girl, a feminist I knew, had done this and when the baby was a boy, she had given the horrible thing away to try again for a girl. This offended me. There was always talk of how to conceive without having to go near a man. IVF wasn't an option for me even if it did become available to us. I still believed a child should have the security of a marriage. Even if I wasn't lesbian I would never contemplate marriage to anyone other than a Christian man. They were different in my opinion; they had God to at least try to keep them honest and loving.

My nostalgia had me hire out the old tapes from the teaching series by Judson Cornwall on Song of Songs. I could still hear the gentle, intimate call of Jesus in the tapes. I listened to them all. I remembered the love I had felt for Greg and it seemed that this sort of love belonged to someone other than me. I even prayed for him that God would bless him. I couldn't pray for myself. I had never really forgotten him. The years had made him the more pure in my memory and me the more scum-like. I doubted heaven could hear me now anyway. I was too far away.

I tried revisiting my old church, which was now meeting in the Town Hall. I sat up in a front row with some of my old friends, Geoff and Karen. Unfortunately just the week before, I had renewed acquaintance with one of my first old lovers, a girl I called "the lady Adie". She was fast becoming a political Maori activist with her sharp, intelligent mind. She had wanted me to meet her for a poetry night. I had promised to meet her at a certain time and this meant I had to get up and leave the church service in the middle of the sermon.

People told me years after that they remembered seeing this butch-looking woman in her heavy clothes, leather jacket and cropped hair, getting up, walking out with such a staunch attitude. A larger than life perception. I had a plastic bomber jacket and a very embarrassed, timid attitude seeing all those straight people. I had enjoyed the service but it was now so foreign to me that I couldn't see how I would ever get back.

Sharon was now living in Auckland. I played along with her to let her think I was still in love with her while trying to conjure up some way of hurting her. She was playing into my scheme when it backfired and she spurned me in front of her friends. This added insult. I would have no recourse but to see her dead. I tried to find one of my enemies to convince them to kill Sharon for payment. Fortunately I wasn't rich enough and no one took me seriously.

I looked more closely at Sharon. Why was she like she was? I now knew a lot about her life and the hurts of her own childhood. She and I were now the same. I was just as dead as she had been when we first started. At last I understood. She could only have destroyed me as she did because she was already destroyed. Now I felt nothing but pity. Seeing this, finally, after seven years, I was able to forgive her and walk away.

Chapter 10

In Auckland, it was more difficult to continue my liberal attitude toward relationships. Auckland girls didn't operate this
way and I could get into some trouble being too promiscuous.
I settled with Dot. She was the most masculine woman I had
ever met, but gentle and genuine. She worked in the heavy
trucking division of a trucks parts warehouse. Often men
would ring up and ask for help to fix their trucks. They were
perplexed when Dot turned up and more astounded when she
could fix the problem. Other guys would turn up at home on
Saturdays to get her to help fix their motorbikes.

Without the hope of lasting love we took yet another flat.
She was very independent and found living with anyone hard.
I was not totally happy as her sturdy, stocky cat beat up my cats
and drove one away for good. At least my chubby little stray
with the stunted tail put up with the abuse and stayed with me.

When Dot wanted to sell her motorbike and buy a small
house on Waiheke Island, I let her go. Our relationship was
dearer if we were apart and it freed me to continue keeping
my options open. I wasn't unhappy. I had a new kitten too,
Yowlie. Cats were more loyal than people and gave more
unqualified affection. All they wanted in return was food and
mutual company.

I had other girls, some whom I had known for years. I
wasn't keen on living alone. I could do it but I preferred having someone there. Sometimes I would go over and stay with
Dot at her island home. The arrangement suited us best. I
understood her more than she realized. I had no intention of
binding anyone. I was way beyond that.

I had learned too that clinging to anyone only drove them away. Sometimes telling them to "Get out!" had them running back. It was the old story, wanting whatever you can't have with more fervour than appreciating what is already there.

Dot taught me a lot. I loved to hear her stories of her childhood and how her family had made ends meet, living close to the swamps in the countryside. She would tell me of her father's drinking and how they never had any money. Of how her mother had died when she was a teenager. How she had married to try to honour her mother and the disaster this had been. When I listened I would wonder why she didn't fix any blame for her own woes on her parents. To my mind they had failed her.

When Dot listened to my moaning and bewailing of my parents, she would chide me. Why was I always blaming my parents? I had no right to their support. I had long ago left their nest. What was it to me what was in the past? They probably had done what they thought was best for me. Had I ever considered what they'd given me?

She forced me to look at my attitudes. If she could look over her shoulder and hold no blame for her parents, then why was I doing this? Dot said, "You're responsible for your own life. No one can make you unhappy. Only you can. Why don't you give up holding all those grudges? Your parents are just people like you. They made mistakes. So what? What sort of mistakes have you made?"

I was losing ground. If I couldn't keep on blaming my parents, then I would have to make some changes in my own thinking. She had the right to tell me off and I let it change me. For the first time in my life, I let go of blaming everyone behind me. My parents, Sharon, Anne, Anne's American lover, all Americans, men in general, my bosses. From now on, what I made of life was my choice and I alone could accept accountability for it.

Forgiveness of Sharon had been my first major release. Letting go of blame was the next. Never again would I expect my parents to carry me or blame them for not carrying me. Whatever was going to be for me and my life, was my decision.

Then one night I made the mistake of taking a girl home who was a sincere, kind person. She had only ever been in one other long-term relationship and had been very hurt. I didn't have the heart to treat her like something shabby. Before I knew it I was the new girlfriend. Perhaps I could make it work. This was the kind of person I had been looking for all these years and yet now that I was with Lilly I couldn't summon up anything in me to return the compliment.

I stayed over a year but it became more of a pretence every day. As much as I cared about her, I couldn't stay. A more niggling urge was to try to get back to God. It was an annoying niggle because I didn't believe that I could.

One day when I was at home alone, there was a knock at the door. Two Christians from a local church were standing there. They assured me that they were solely visiting to see what sorts of needs were in their neighbourhood. I was impressed. I asked them in to continue filling in their survey.

They were very approachable and caring and I found myself explaining that I was a backslidden Christian. They were firm, telling me I needed to get my life right with God but they also prayed with me. It felt very odd. As they left, I watched them walking away looking so straight. How could I ever go back and be part of that? I shook my head. Only God knew.

It was a catalyst for moving out of my last real relationship. If I was ever to get back to God, I couldn't do it if I was tied.

I had left my job at the wholesale tour company. They were discriminating against me with pay and perks. Younger, less-experienced people were sent overseas and I stayed back to work the job. I thought it was because I was lesbian, but in hindsight it probably had far more to do with my general demeanour and my drinking habits. They couldn't have sent someone like me with the obvious drinking problem that I had, to meet and guide tours in Disneyland.

What they hadn't realized was that although I was a drunk, I was also a hard worker. Out of the 55 groups we had on the go between three workers in the department, 51 of them were being organized and run by me. Was it my fault I made the work look easy?

I quit the job and laughed when they realized this loss. It was cold comfort because I now wondered why my life was targeted by anyone who wanted to take advantage of me. I had put my heart and soul into this job, to have something to live for, and my job had knifed me as skilfully as any lover.

I said goodbye to Lilly and moved into another house with two gay men friends. The thorn in the flesh in this house was the landlord who would arrive and come in at any hour he wanted to. He disliked my cats; I now had four. He was sure I was damaging his house with the Mini Minor car I used for work. He hated the colours we had painted our rooms and was threatening to throw us out. He later sued me for damage and won, even though he had already made this same claim on the previous tenants.

I was now working in retail travel, the direction I had aimed at for my career. I had worked a year as a senior consultant in a suburban agency, gripping the chair with nerves, and now I was managing a small agency in another suburb. There were two of us in the office and I had learnt the managerial art of "going out". My junior did most of the work.

I loved this travel business. I didn't seem to get the trips like others did, but I still enjoyed the nature of the job. Information changed every day; it was hopeless to attempt to know everything that could be known. There was always another course to attain and levels of qualifications. I worked the ten-year requirement and qualified to the level of Travel Management.

With this dream job came long hours and low pay. This meant less to me than a boring job. I had by now tasted some other countries, the USA, Fiji, all of New Zealand by coach and of course, my beloved Sydney.

Trying to keep up my womanizing was starting to get boring but what else could I do? Wine, woman and song, dance and the races. I had my hobbies.

Our landlord had his way. We were booted out. I had flatted with enough people by now. Most of what I had owned of any value had been stolen over the years by flatmates or their friends. It was far less hassle to live alone. I had done it once before and now it was the only alternative.

I took a flat in Herne Bay, Auckland, again near the inner city. It was a tiny flat in the back of an old wooden, dilapidated villa. The flat itself was newly decorated since gang members had last rented it and had trashed the inside. They still had a key, I was informed. I changed the lock. It was clean and perfect for my needs. It was also damp, but then most of my flats had been damp. People on travel wages didn't earn enough for the luxury of a dry flat.

I had seen a bit of Jasmine and I still saw Dot, and I still saw two other "friends" along with attempts to conquer "one nighters". But life was very empty. I started to look back over the years. I couldn't remember one weekend from the last. They all merged into one boring line of weekends of drink and parties, all dull and meaningless.

When I moved into my new flat I didn't want anyone to know where I lived. It would be my haven. I didn't even want any lovers there. I wanted to be a hermit. However there was one new lover whom I had just met, Hydra. She was into New Age and the occult and had sometimes frequented covens. She wasn't keen on letting me remain independent and came to my home. I wasn't happy about anyone pinning me down but she was becoming very possessive. The movie *Fatal Attraction* was out and I was starting to see some similarities.

This didn't fit my pattern of outrunning the devil. I was supposed to be the winner. This girl was like no one else I had known in the scene. Even my old friends thought she must be possessed. They warned me not to get involved. Too late. I couldn't detach her. I would go out and come back late Saturday night to find she had smashed my door window to get in and she would be waiting for me with venom blazing in her eyes.

"Where've you been?" she would hiss.

She threatened to kill my cats. No one touched my cats! I could talk my way through to save myself, but I was scared to come home one day and find one of my cats sacrificed on the doorstep. She would have been bound to pick Yowlie, my favourite, or Blossom, my chubby, endearing, half-tailed friend. Blossom had been more faithful to me than anyone I had ever known. Women came and went, but my cats loved me forever.

I couldn't dare to see Jasmine for fear of what Hydra would do. I didn't dare go over to Dot for a while for fear of a furry massacre. Maybe the time had come to commit suicide. Jumping from the Harbour Bridge would be an option but there was no guarantee I would die. I might just be mutilated. I could take pills. A girl I knew in Sydney had done this. Nagging in the background of my mind was the possibility that hell was on the other side. I certainly couldn't repent of suicide and there was no assurance that I could rely on getting to heaven. That they both existed was still a probability.

One night I had been at a gay nightclub and was minding my own business sitting out a dance, downing a refreshment, when a sudden thought came. "What if Jesus returned tonight?" I was chilled to the marrow. Then I thought, "If he did, and even if it meant that I personally went to hell, I would welcome it." It would mean an end to all of this and Jesus was still the best in my books, whether I deserved him or not.

Work had dropped off and the company was thinking of selling my office. My slack efforts on the job had run the business down. The job was over. I was out looking for work again and there had just been a reduction of staff at Air New Zealand. Dozens of qualified agents were looking for work. Did I have fifteen years experience? No? Then I might as well forget finding a job. Maybe my reputation had gone before me. I doubted my old bosses would have had much to applaud me for.

The thing I was best known for was being the last to leave at every function. As long as there was free drink and someone to drink with, I would still be there. In my industry I could go to functions every week if I wanted to. Some of my workmates had started to point out to me that I might have a drinking problem.

I wasn't ready to accept that yet. The alternative was that I would have to face society without drink. I still couldn't see how I might have a drinking problem when I didn't drink every day. The quantities I drank meant little. I had been on medication once and it required giving up alcohol. In the end, I put up with the muscle pain and went back to the drink. This had concerned me a little. Maybe I couldn't give it up?

Now I was out of work and searching for anything. I still had to pay my rent. I could get by with little food. Many times I had lived on two meals per week. I could do this again. There was a little temp work but life was getting more aggravating.

The evil I saw looking at me through Hydra reminded me of the exorcisms I had seen and experienced back in the days when demons were being expelled from my hippie friends. This reminded me of the power of God.

Chapter 11

I found a little temp work. It was just keeping me going. One night I was walking up Queen Street. It was the day that Israel had invaded Lebanon and had annihilated the PLO. I felt like I was waiting, with the enemy crouched close at my borders on every side too. It was checkmate. I could throw in the game and die. This was most logical. Yet there was still this God to consider. If he was out there ...

It was an ordinary Tuesday night in early autumn. I had often prayed this prayer but I prayed it again, muttering as I walked up Queen Street to catch my bus home: "God, if you're out there, and I'm starting to wonder if you are, is there some way I can get back to you? If there is, please give me a sign. I don't expect a big neon sign, because I know this is wrong.[6] But if you just show me I can get back to you, then I will know it's possible." I didn't add it but there was only one alternative.

I never had food in the house. In the fridge there might be a little milk for tea or coffee and that would be about all. I bought lunch if I was working and lived off potatoes or whatever I could scrounge from my parents as I visited each week. At least I could get a meal there once a week. It was a common evening meal for me to boil a potato and while I was waiting for it to cook, I would eat a liquorice strap. This seemed normal to me and nutritious since the liquorice had iron and the potato vitamin C, as long as I left the skins on. About once a week I would buy Chinese takeaways if I could afford them, so that I ate a healthy diet! Just now and then I would cook something, just to be healthy, and tonight I had just had a small meal when there was a knock at my door.

I was a bit wary that it could be Hydra as there was barely anyone else who knew where I lived. But my weekdays were sacred and I normally only saw her at weekends. I opened the door to see a tall, lean man whom I recognized as Geoff Day. I had known him when I was a hippie Christian and had last seen him when I had visited the Town Hall church service a year or so before. I assumed he must have been going door-to-door with his gospel message.

"Can I come in?"

"Sure."

I made us a pot of tea and Geoff settled himself on the odd couch I had made from an old stretcher.

"I'll be honest with you," said my gentle friend. "I was sent here by the church."

I nodded for him to go on.

"Your mother's been worried about you and contacted our church a few weeks ago. Your sister did too. I've waited until tonight to come and see you."

My mother? She hated this church; it was Pentecostal. Besides with 2,000 people to look after already, why would the church bother with a wayward woman who had no intention of contacting them?

"So you felt right about coming tonight?"

"Yes. I was asked to, since I'm the home group leader for this area."

I had my sign. Eyeing Geoff up I remembered that he was probably the most discreet individual I ever knew. I would be safe pouring out my heart to him. It was time to come clean. Totally clean.

Geoff knew my lifestyle. I didn't need to tell him about this. Lesbianism was only a symptom of a deeper infection. My real sin, my so far hidden sin, was the first disobedience.

Because Geoff knew the people I had known in my earlier years, I was able to be totally open with him. I told him about how God had given me clear direction to go to the church in Christchurch. I told him how I had felt about Greg and how this had rendered me paralyzed with fear at the thought of ever seeing him again; how I had been lied to about his engagement and how, despite God's clear word, I had refused to obey because of this. I would not trust God with my fear.

Now I had explored life to the full extent of my own soul's choices. I had withheld from myself no pleasure or fulfilment that was within my power to have.[7] If God would give me another chance I would walk in his ways to the end of my life.

I talked for hours and Geoff graciously listened. I felt free for the first time in eight and a half years. At the end of the evening Geoff got up to go.

"Would you like it if Karen and I came and picked you up for church on Sunday?"

"Sure."

I learned afterwards that Geoff had come with trepidation. He had fully expected me to kick him down the path with a few expletives. My easy agreement to come to church sent him on his way elated.

I had my sign. If God was reaching out to me, then I could get back! I mulled it over. If this was another chance I couldn't blow it. This was probably my only shot at getting back to Jesus. I would have to make a hard, cold decision to walk in his ways whether I ever knew another day of joy and happiness or not. I decided to radically amputate everything behind me. From now on, I would determine to only go where the Lord led me, or do what he wanted.

On Friday, the gay pub was shutting its doors. It was the last night for any of us to be able to drink at this temple of booze worship. This fact didn't escape me. I would never have to know where everyone chose to drink in the future and there was no temptation to go back to this old pub.

I went for the final night. It was a party atmosphere and I shouted a few jugs to say my own goodbyes.

"Where're you going?"

"Back to God," I answered.

"Don't be ridiculous, no one just leaves! You'll be back!"

"I won't, you know."

Two of my friends, and Hydra was one, were incredulous. They had to know more. I began there and then to share Jesus with them.

After the pub I went to a nightclub to find other friends to say goodbye, then to a party. I covered as many as I could, shouting drinks and making my farewell.

On Saturday I recovered from the drinking binge, had a quiet early night and rose to go to church on Sunday morning.

Geoff and Karen arrived and we went to the service. I wore a grey work suit, blouse and skirt. I wanted to blend in and be unnoticed. I was finding my first morning back a little depressing. There was no turning back now. I slipped into the seat and the service began. Unfortunately for me, two of the pastors knew me. One was waving and smiling; the other drew attention to me with a personal welcome. I could have shrunk under the seat but it was nice to be welcomed all the same.

In the foyer I bumped into an old boyfriend. He said in the first few sentences, "The Lord isn't going to make it easy for you to get back, you know!"

I snapped at him. "Don't you know how hard it's already been? I've been trying to get back for over eight years. But I'm back now!"

This Christian thing was hard work.

I went back to my flat and the loneliness set in at once. What had I done? My Christian friends were now older and married. They had homes to go to. I didn't know any Christian singles and I had cut off my past bridges. I stared at the walls until Monday.

My sister was my mainstay. She had prayed me back and now she had her new role, encouraging me, collecting the woeful phone calls crying out for help. I had to have a lifeline; I was never going back. No matter how hard and depressing this was, what was behind me was worse.

I had cut back a little on my vices but I wasn't going to let go of anything simply because it was expected of Christians. I would only do it if God pointed it out.

Smoking had dropped off immediately. I never bothered with another cigarette or any other substance, from the first Sunday onward. But drink was another matter. Jesus drank. I could control it, I argued, but the Lord would deal with this one in his time.

After a few weeks I became painfully aware of how much I had failed God. I prayed and started to spiral down with condemnation. Then I heard the quiet voice of Jesus say to me, "Do you think that I loved you when you were away from me?" I had to accept that he did, otherwise he would never have brought me back to himself. "Then what makes you think that I love you any less, now that you have come back?" He had me there.

There were many endings to my old story, and a whole new life to live. I talked to Jasmine on the phone but I never saw her again. She said that she loved me. I said I loved her too and because of that, I wished she could know Jesus. Along with others, I still pray for Jasmine to know Jesus. Wherever she is, I could think of nothing more wonderful than if she found real love as I have done.

One day I was praying in general for my friends when Sharon's name came to mind. Suddenly I was weeping for her soul. When the tears subsided I was amazed. Surely this was God's heart, not mine. I thought Sharon had gone too far. She had literally turned her back on God, blaspheming, turning to the occult. She had gone even further away than I had. Now the Holy Spirit was giving me motivation to pray, so there had to be hope even for her.

Not many days after this, I heard a knock at my door in the early hours of the morning. It was Sharon. She had a black eye and was in a mess. I let her in. How she knew where I lived, I had no idea. Very few people knew my new flat.

She was in another violent relationship. She had been beaten up. She had decided to do the old hippie trail through Asia and blow her brains out on drugs. There was no other way to go on. I told her, "Yes there is! Look at me! Why don't you come back to Jesus too?" She said she would think about it.

Could she stay this night? Sure, she would have to share my bed. It wasn't a wonderful bed either; I had learned to sleep between the wire spikes that had made their way up from the torn mattress. Her side was less comfortable with spikes in the wrong places, but she was a little "out of it" and probably wouldn't notice.

The thought flickered through my mind. Wasn't this what I had waited for those seven years, my moment to crucify Sharon? What of my old feelings for her? There were none. All I could feel was compassion and a love that was God's love. I wanted more than anything to convince her to come back to God as I had.

In the morning she said, "Funny, I have been watching you for years. What you had that attracted me was lost, but you have it back now."

"Yes, Sharon. It's Jesus."

"Maybe."

We talked some more. She was contrite about our old relationship. She admitted that even before the fateful night in Christchurch, she had felt the same way about me as I had about her. This gave me some comfort. I had always taken all the blame. Now I could let that go too.

As she left, she promised to think about what I had said.

A few days later she had a major bike accident. She had travelled at high speed in the early hours of the morning on her 750 motorbike, through a red light. It was a main intersection and she hit a car. She would have died then and there but there was a woman jogger who happened to be there right on the spot. This jogger said she was a doctor and she kept Sharon alive until the ambulance arrived. No one ever traced this doctor. Her name was unknown to anyone.

A blood clot was removed from Sharon's brain in the early hours of the morning and her family were told that she would probably not live or if she did, she would be severely brain-damaged for the rest of her life. Her parents flew to Auckland. Sharon had won her mother and stepfather to the Lord in her earlier days as a Christian.

I never saw such faith. They stoically waited at the bedside trusting the Lord. Gradually Sharon came out of the coma, but she came out cursing God. Her friends were astounded that she had made a miraculous recovery. Sharon was unimpressed and as her health returned, she went straight back to her old life.

Her parents returned to Wellington and I wrote to them, wanting to comfort them in what must surely have been a sore disappointment. No, on the contrary, her mother wrote back praising God for his miraculous healing and she added that they were now just waiting for the inevitable return Sharon would make back to Jesus. I was humbled and knew God had to see faith like this!

Sharon went back to secondary school teaching and many years later wrote to me asking how I had come back to the Lord. She was starting to make her way back.

Making my own way back with the Lord was a therapy that I had to take like "cold turkey". Nights I sat in my flat, alone, knowing there was a party only one street away with my old friends. I would cling on to my Christian tapes or play old worship songs I had kept over the years. Sometimes I would go out of town and stay with my sister on the farm where she lived.

For a time the Lord let me think that I was a celibate lesbian. I didn't think I could ever see myself as straight. I tried to keep in contact with many of my old friends because I wanted to win them to Jesus. News of my departure from my lifestyle was big gossip for a long time. Everyone I met up with had heard. They were unbelieving. No one did this. Some, however, said that they were glad for me since I had been such a mess.

The habit thinking took a while to go. I found out about two lesbian girls who had come to the Lord a year before. I hunted them down, partly because I wanted like company. When I met up with them they could talk of nothing but Jesus. I was grateful as it had exposed my stupidity. I had gone over thinking I could wallow in some "good old days" chat.

This experience reminded me of when Monica and I had gone to Sydney. When we got there I noticed that ex-Kiwis lived mostly in a couple of inner city suburbs, Bondi having the biggest concentration. We could have fitted straight into a ghetto of ex-Kiwis. I didn't want to do this and my aim was to assimilate as quickly as possible into the new culture. I wanted to only have Australian friends, live in areas where there were few Kiwis and to become part of the new land.

Coming back to the kingdom of God, I had made a similar commitment. I wanted to be able to speak the kingdom language, not that I mean "Christianese", but find what it meant to speak and ask and live in this community. If I had ghettoed with ex-gays, this would have made it far more difficult. I wanted to quickly remove the vestiges of my old lifestyle. When people tell me that they can't see anything but Jesus and a Christian woman when they meet me, I feel great. I have become a "local" in his kingdom.

One day I had borrowed an old friend's car and was driving into town. I saw a gorgeous-looking young girl walking along the footpath. I did what I had often done and leaned out the window and whistled. Then I turned back to face the road. Immediately I was aware that there was another presence in the car. I had Jesus in the passenger seat. I couldn't see him, but I knew without a doubt he was there! I flushed with mortification. There was no condemnation, just a strong revelation of my absurdity. The celibate homosexual label dropped from me like a stone. I was as God had made me, a woman. I had better start getting used to it.

Because of what I had been through, I had no desire to go back. I had no doubt that sin was death and that there was no greener pasture than the pasture of my good shepherd. Before me was a hope and a future. Behind me was the smell of my singed life as I had passed by the edge of hell. I had seen what I was capable of, left to my godforsaken nature. I had also learned that the devil never tempts anyone with the impossible. There is no safe fantasy.

I never wanted to look back over my shoulder. For this reason and because my parents had never known about my life, I vowed I would never tell my story until they were gone. Also, I didn't want the label "ex-gay" to define me.

Living alone, I spent a lot of time in prayer and re-reading and studying the Bible. It was all fresh and I was so hungry. I devoured teaching tapes and sang, not melancholic love songs, but new worship songs I had written just for Jesus.

My cats were slow to respond to this new person at first. Yowlie, true to her name, would meow in wailing, pleading tones every time I sang. With a look of contempt, she would flee out the door. Blossom, on the other hand, would try to climb to my face and would bat at my lips gently with her soft white paws. I decided she had been converted too, and that we had to work on Yowlie and the other two cats.

As summer came in this year of my return, I would go down to the bay at the end of my road. I would take my Bible and sit up on the cliff bank until the sun went low. Jesus was becoming the intimate love I had looked for all my life. The love of my life, just as he had first shown himself to me through the Song of Songs.

One evening I was reading Song of Songs. I came to the description of the king. "My lover is radiant and ruddy. Outstanding among ten thousand. His head is purest gold; his hair is wavy and black as a raven."

Looking up I saw a young man who had arrived at the beach alone. His body was honed and as he disrobed to swim, I could see his flawless figure.

I went back to the Bible. "His arms are rods of gold set with chrysolite. His body is like polished ivory decorated with sapphires." The fair but dark-haired man continued to take off all his clothes, oblivious of my presence on the cliff. Perhaps he didn't care.

"His legs are pillars of marble set on bases of pure gold." The young man waded naked into the sea as the sun threw gold light across the rippled mirror. He kept wading until he was able to spread his arms and swim out into the bay, heading toward the sinking sun. "His appearance is like Lebanon, choice as its cedars."

"OK, Lord, very graphic. I get the picture." I had to laugh as I gathered my Bible under my arm and headed back up the path. "My beloved is mine and I am his." No other could compare to my Lord. No one had loved me as he had done. No one had shown such acceptance, no one such long-suffering and patience.

I had gone where the prophetic utterance at the end of Bible College had warned me not to go, but I was back now. I could hope for a new life. Perhaps I had forfeited the prophesies through disobedience? Could I ever overcome my fear of the public eye and be a bride? I doubted I would ever love anyone as I had loved Greg and doubted I could ever love a man. However, time would reveal another story yet to open.

Part 2

The Taming
of the Shirl

When I found my peace with God and returned to following him with my whole heart, I had no illusions that I could continue in my old lifestyle. My experience of Jesus was such that there was no doubt that the two lifestyles were as incompatible as jam and garlic, or pickled onions and ice cream.

I had heard others say that they could be Christian and gay, but to me my relationship with Jesus was not something academic or mystical. For me, to continue in my lesbian lifestyle and include Jesus would be as offensive as expecting a husband to accept the inclusion of an old lover. I had to leave my old lover, the lifestyle I had been living, and espouse myself to Jesus. Any idol that was higher than him would have to topple.

However, I doubted I would ever be able to love a male, and as I had no longer any intention of searching for love in another woman, I assumed my life from this point would be one of celibacy. I wasn't too concerned as I felt as if I had "burned out" on passion. I doubted I had anything left in my emotions to be whole in a relationship anyway. So I just left it at that and worked on trying to find my feet as a follower of God.

God had a plan already and it did include a man, but not one I would readily notice and certainly not a romance as I had known romance before. This was an arranged marriage and my heavenly Father was organizing the event. Through it I would learn a lot about love.

In the meantime, I had to slowly work my way back into a decent job. It would take some time to regain a good reputation. At the point that I had committed myself to walk in God's ways, no matter what, I was out of work. But I was also living alone in a little unit in an inner city suburb and I had rent to pay.

Temporary jobs came up for a few weeks and I would manage to buy a little bread, pay my rent and feed my four cats. Then I would have days and sometimes a week or two with no work and no pay. This became a subject for prayer in my early days of learning to trust God.

Having drunk away most of my earlier earnings I was without a car and living in a one bedroomed flat that had been sectioned off within an old villa. At the back of this rather run-down house with the paint bleached and peeling from the weatherboards, was my little home. It contained a damp bedroom, a small living room, bathroom and tiny kitchen. Next to my flat was a grubby little flat with a tiny bedroom and even tinier living area. At least mine had been newly painted.

I had an old double bed that had been given to me. It might have been better to sleep on the floor as the wire weave was sagged and the mattress was old and musty. Hard, coiled springs were poking through in various places and I had learned to sleep between them so that I didn't get scratched.

For a couch, I owned an old army stretcher with old, folded curtains for cushions, covered by a large piece of material. Two old chairs with cane woven backs and woven, faded seats were the only other items to sit on. I had a small coffee table, an old three-in-one stereo and, my largest piece of furniture, a huge fish tank sitting on a board and three heavy concrete bricks. My cats had been trained not to look at this fish tank as "looking was temptation", a good reminder to me as I went about the city. To complete this rustic scene was a bookshelf made of concrete bricks and long boards.

As a drunk, I had never been fussy about housework or household pride but in the year before I returned to Jesus, I was becoming fed up with my sloppy habits and had become almost fastidious, despite my meagre possessions. I busied myself each weekend scrubbing the little kitchen floor, washing windows and keeping everything in its place.

Travel, as an industry, was not known for high pay, especially at the level I worked, so life was always basic for me. I knew the best charity shops to buy work clothes and was expert at making a pair of laddered stockings last way past their use by date.

When I had work, I would catch the bus, work the day and then return to my little home. If I had enough money I would feed my cats. Once in a while I simply didn't have enough money and couldn't bring myself to go home to see their faces and ignore their pleas. I would stay at an old friend's instead. By the next night, I would have scraped something together for them even if I went hungry.

My life to date had been one of endless parties and nightclubbing and now I would return to the silence of my home and wait for the next day's work. On Fridays I would say goodbye to my workmates and sit at home, waiting until I was collected by a couple from the church to go to the morning service. Here, although I was among the huge congregation, I mostly just spoke to the couple I had arrived with and then I would be dropped home. The next human I would interact with would be my workmate on a Monday morning, if I had work.

Soon I was attending a mid-week Christian meeting in my area. This was a "lifeblood" night for me as it represented my new social life. Here were people from half-way houses with various disabilities, a couple who played in the symphonia, a model, a wharfie, an elderly couple and a few others who seemed more conventional. Then there was me, the ex-lesbian.

The first night I attended this group, the couple who had been so instrumental in bringing me back to relationship with Jesus had brought me to a homely house in my suburb. It was mid-winter and a fire crackled in the hearth in the living room.

I was ushered in and we were early. There was just one other young man standing in the room. My friends went into the kitchen to excitedly share with the home owners about how great it was that I had come along, not that I knew this. So, I was left with the one other early comer. He looked at me with an intense gaze, took my hand and announced in a long flat monotone, "Hi, my name is Clayton. I guess the Lord will heal me of my schizophrenia one day."

For a moment terror gripped me. I had never been anywhere socially for at least eight years without first being fortified with alcohol. It wasn't that schizophrenia in itself was a problem to me; after all, my own brother had been autistic. It was just meeting anyone at all, let alone someone making this blunt declaration so early in my evening. My mind screamed, "Get me out of here! I just want a cold beer and some familiar company!"

The door opened and a second person entered the room. I relaxed for a moment and then recognized this woman. I had known her years before when I had attended church as a young girl. Of all people, how could this dragon of a woman be part of this home group meeting? I thought she lived on the other side of town but here she was. I had an aversion to this woman, as she had been particularly critical of me as a teenager. She had caused me no end of pain as she had lambasted me for my clothing.

In Lottie's opinion my clothes had been offensive: too short, too tight, too ungodly, and she had ensured that I was sent to the pastor for discipline. He had laughed and told me he had more problems with old ladies like Lottie than with my clothes, but she had hounded me to tears and now this pinched-faced, wizened old bat was part of my home group!

I recalled the time when she had made me go with her to

a school, to observe her taking "Bible-in-Schools". When I arrived she told me that I was taking a class of eleven and twelve year olds for half an hour. I had no material and it was class Double-D-minus-semi-epsilon-moron-craft class. They were abnormally big for their age too.

I was thrown through the door to the wolves on the other side who started to throw paper at me and pull each other's hair. It was the "Bash Street Gang" and no mistake. There was only one thing I could do in the circumstances. Ignoring my terror of public speaking, I preached my sole hell-fire and damnation message. I preached solidly for the whole half-hour, hardly daring to breathe between sentences. It seemed to work because they sat in rapt attention. At the end of half an hour Lottie came back to rescue me. The kids loved it! They all wanted to carry my bag.

Lottie had scowled at me and made a comment about the way I had gone to the school in a coat dress! A coat dress! I had not forgotten this old lady! Was God crazy letting her come tonight?

Within seconds I realized that she didn't recognize me at all. This was one blessing and I wasn't about to fill her in with our previous acquaintance. I just made a mental note to keep my distance from Lottie, and Clayton.

The second week I went to the group I was in a hurry before leaving home. I had been making an effort to wear more feminine clothing and this night I had put on a brown skirt that had layers of material. I looked in the mirror and realized that it needed an iron, partly because I could hear Mrs Wilson's voice floating in from the past admonishing me, but I had run out of time. I thought, "Lottie will frown disapprovingly and say, 'Your skirt is un-ironed'" and I planned that I would retort, "And your tongue is unbridled!" I was not going to let anyone walk over me ever again.

Sure enough, as I sat in the meeting, Lottie was inspecting my skirt. I was ready. The programme ended and we went into the dining area for a cup of coffee. Lottie lost no time and came to her target straightaway. She said, "You know, Shirley, I have been looking at your skirt all evening."

In my mind I rehearsed the line, "And your tongue is unbridled."

"Yes," she continued, "and I have been thinking what a pretty skirt that is. I wish I had one like that!"

A large chip dropped off my shoulder as I spluttered to find an appropriate reply. When I shut the door in my own home, I said to the Lord, "Only you knew."

A few weeks later the Lord gave me a chance to deepen my lesson and actually learn how to love this old lady. By now I had realized that she had changed dramatically in the twelve years since I had known her. The hardness had gone and she loved nothing better than to encourage people with the many scriptures she had memorized.

One week she came into the group and I noticed she had a rather large abscess on her face. It had been growing for a while and I could see it was distressing her. Then I felt like the Lord said to me, "If you will go one more step and give this old lady a hug, pouring all your love into her, then as you do, I will heal her." So I did. The next week she returned and the abscess was totally gone along with any of my earlier disparagement of this lovely old saint.

Dress was an issue for me. I tried to leave behind anything that hinted of my past. I wore skirts and dresses a lot. I was always in another charity shop looking for something a little more feminine but had little idea and often my clothes were strange mismatches.

Rediscovering the Lord was like being in a spiritual hothouse. I was shut in with him, as he was my only close companion. I rediscovered one old friend, Loran, who lived across the harbour. We met to renew our friendship and she stood by me as I refound my feet. The people in the home group were becoming very dear to me, but there was no one amongst them who was single and compatible to have as a friend.

My most regular friend from the group was a young girl in her early twenties. I was 28. However, this girl had a mental age of around nine. She lived in a little bedsit room at the end of my street and she would visit me at the weekends.

Now, instead of partying with a hoard of rowdy old friends, I would sit and play monopoly with Dinah and the worst part was that she would win every time. She also had a real gift for plucking weird ideas out of the air and finding things I had lost. I would be huffing and puffing and trying to find a book or some such item and she would say, "Have you looked under the fish tank?" And there it would be.

The dark and dank little flat next to mine provided the other regular visitor. As soon as I returned to the Lord, a young man with a drinking problem moved into this flat. I was not averse to having the odd drink as I had decided that unless the Lord put his finger on any of my activities, I was not going to get religious or legalistic and give anything up.

Leaving drugs behind and burning my porn magazines was understood. However, Jesus drank wine and it didn't seem quite so obvious as to whether drink was acceptable or not. I figured drunkenness was out but I imagined this would not be a problem to me as I was going to try to be good in this area.

About two weeks after the alcoholic neighbour had moved in, he paid a convivial call with a dozen beers. It was a Sunday morning and this was a bit early for me, even for my earlier days. He was very friendly and, I could tell, a bit lonely, so in the end, I agreed to one can. This went down. Then the next and as the afternoon went on another dozen appeared and these too were consumed. As usual, once the second can had hit my beer gland a dozen were a reasonably casual number for me to remain sober but perhaps be just a little affected.

Suddenly it was time for the evening service and I remembered that I had invited one of my old friends to church. There was no way I was going to stand Hydra up as I cared about her soul and wanted her to come to know Jesus. I leaped up and said goodbye, grabbing my bag. I locked my flat and hurried to the bus.

When I met my friend I was feeling pretty mellow and we made our way into the balcony of the Town Hall where the church met. For the first time since I had been back to church, I felt comfortable about singing with all my heart. With the alcohol for fortification, I felt uninhibited and for the first time in many years, I raised my hands to the Lord.

Suddenly I felt as if I was going to black out. I had to get out right away! I excused myself to my friend and rushed for the Town Hall foyer. There I managed to get to a marble step and sit down. A security guard came over and asked if I was OK.

"No," I groaned. "I'm going to be sick."

He had just enough time to get a long square metal ashtray to me, and I fulfilled my promise! I couldn't believe it. I wasn't even drunk! A crate was normal; I didn't even feel inebriated. Here I sat in astonishment and full realization that the booze and worshipping the Lord didn't mix.

Sitting like a gutter dweller on the fine-worn marble steps, I was glad the entrance to this prestigious building was empty of people, apart from the bemused security guard. Just then a large Polynesian woman and her European husband came in. The woman scurried over to me and wrapped a big warm, motherly arm around me.

"Oh, dear," she crooned. "Are you alright?"

"Yes," I said meekly, the fumes of the alcohol surrounding me.

"I think you might have a problem with the alcohol, eh?" she probed.

"Yes," I admitted for the first time in my life.

"I'll pray for you."

She prayed a loving, firm prayer that I would be released from the hold of alcohol and healed of my addiction. I immediately felt lighter.

"You betta go see a pastor, I think, and get him to pray for you to set you free," she advised.

I nodded feeling very humbled and rather stupid. Right now I just wanted to get away from the ashtray. The woman and her husband moved on into the auditorium as I went to the bathroom. As I stood, I watched her go and thought, "Hey, I am free! I won't need to go to the pastor. Your prayer has set me free." But the couple had melted into the huge congregation and I never noted this woman again. But I was indeed free.

Before this point, I had never been able to stop drinking once I started; I just kept my elbow bending. I would drink other people's drinks, drink men under the table – I was a "hero of the drink" and fitted the biblical description in the book of Proverbs exactly.[8] I marvelled at people who could have a glass of wine and that was all that they wanted. For me, the first glass just formed the initial layer and the feeling of drunkenness was a panacea.

Once, I had been given some muscle relaxants for a painful joint problem, but I couldn't take them with alcohol, so after three days, I had put aside the pills and gone back to the drink, preferring the pain to the alcohol deprivation.

From the day I sat on the Town Hall steps, I have never been enslaved to alcohol. I have never touched beer, which had been my undoing. I had already given up spirits years before as their poisons had nearly killed me twice. But now, more of a miracle than to never drink again, I was able to have a glass of wine, and not want any more.

I now have a genuine distaste for feeling affected by alcohol in any way. These days, I may drink a glass about half a dozen times a year with a meal at a special celebration. I have no interest in drinking for socializing; the thought seems to cheapen my relationship with Jesus and quite frankly bores me. I want much more to be filled with the Holy Spirit! And I learned years ago on those cold stone stairs that the two spirits don't mix.

From this landmark day, my neighbour tried valiantly to entice me to drink with him. He came in with cans and asked me to talk about Jesus and offered me drink. He coaxed, cajoled, and while he tried to draw me back to the old gods that he was worshipping, I shared with him about Jesus day after day.

I had begun to love my quiet little flat and the time I now had to myself. I was rediscovering my relationship with Jesus and it was sweet. I couldn't wait to get back from any job I was in, to put on some music and worship, then pray and greedily read the Bible. It was almost like eating rich food. I could taste the words as I filled my soul with them.

Just as I began to read or pray, almost every night this neighbour would knock on my door with his can or bottle and say, "I want to come in."

"Well, it's not a good time."

"You got visitors?"

"No, but I'm just about to pray."

"Yeah, well, I want to talk about God things."

I would let him in and preach to him. But it didn't put him off. I tried getting blunter and blunter and gave him testimonies to read of others who had been set free from drink. But he came back night after night, just at the wrong time, and nothing seemed to be changing.

One night I stopped in mid-sermon and said to him, "Why do you come over all the time, when I just preach at you?"

"Got no telly. It's not so lonely as sitting looking at the four walls."

At this point I prayed after he left, "Lord, if this guy is

going to come to know you, then let it be soon. But if he is just a distraction from spending time with you, then remove him."

By the end of the week he had moved out.

The new neighbour was a dear old soul, Martha, who was schizophrenic. She went from muttering, to wearing eye patches to cover her "evil eye" and poking her false teeth out because an angel had told her that she looked more beautiful this way. She had a few, thin, old blankets and little food. And I loved this little lady. She believed in Jesus. He was her only real and faithful friend.

So now I had two people to spend time with socially: my friend down the road whom I had come to appreciate for her odd skill at finding lost articles and her infuriating luck at Monopoly. And my new neighbour who would come and listen to me read the Bible and eat my strange soups and tell me about her sad life.

How could I be lonely now? God was replacing my good-time friends with some of his most special people. In learning to love them, my own shortcomings seemed to diminish and my lifestyle became less frugal; I felt rich and able to give, since I was better off than they were.

Some of my old friends still dropped in to try to talk me into going out on the town. Some came to ask about what was happening to me. It was news that had spread in the gay scene and everyone had some opinion or other about it. Most wished me well and some added that they had always known that I was a "mess". Religion was good for me but not for them.

The friend I had taken to church came and talked to me. She had come to church because I had met her by chance one day. I had boarded a bus and she was the driver.

"Hmmmm," Hydra had grumbled. "Fancy you getting on my bus today!" She glared at me. I had been a traitor to the lifestyle in her eyes.

"Oh?"

"I had a dream last night and I can't work it out."

"Do tell." I could feel the presence of Jesus as I began to listen.

"I dreamed I was in the coven I used to be in, and we were gloating about something, when all of a sudden, I was pulled down into a dark place. There were these ugly fat babies. That's what they looked like anyway. They were dragging me down deeper into the darkness.

"I began to scream because I could feel that as they dragged me down, the place was getting darker and I could hear people screaming. Then I remembered that when I was a little girl, I gave my life to God, so I started to yell, 'You can't take me because I belong to God.' Then a hand reached down from above and pulled me out of the pit.

"When I was out of the darkness I looked to see who'd rescued me and it was a man in a captain's uniform. It was so weird because I was feeling so great that he had rescued me from the pit and I was really happy, but when I looked into his eyes, he was crying."

"And you don't know what this means?"

"No. It's just freaky. Why would that man have tears in his eyes? You would think he'd be glad he'd rescued me!"

"Do you know that Jesus is called the captain of the host?"[9]

"No. But, hey, if it was Jesus, then why was he so unhappy?"

"This dream was a warning. This is your destiny unless you give your life to Jesus and follow him. His tears were because he doesn't want you to be apart from him in hell for eternity. He wants you to come to him."

My friend accepted Jesus and began to learn about him. However, she had been immersed in the occult for some time and when she began to change from darkness to light, the darkness resented this and worked hard to draw her back. She came down to my flat one night terrified because her bed had begun to levitate. Demonic forces constantly attacked her.

I felt unequipped to help her and struggled to find anyone in the church willing to help disciple my friend. My church held the view that if you repented, every demon would go and there was no need for special prayer for deliverance.

It was also commonly believed that a Christian couldn't be possessed by a demon and possessed by Christ. However, I have noted that people who believe that only a non-believer should have prayer for deliverance would never actually attempt praying for one. So no one ever receives prayer for release from demons, despite this having been a large part of the ministry of Jesus.

However, back in these early days of my faith, I would never personally have attempted praying for anyone to be released from demonic oppression, as I had been taught that this was not something women were allowed to do. Scripture was always quoted that this was because women were deceived. Also that they should be covered from spiritual powers "because of the angels", which they said referred to the fallen angels.[10] The underlying reason for this was that woman, not men, had been deceived in the Garden of Eden, so this also meant they shouldn't deal with spiritual things in this way. None of this held much ground because the logical outcome was that the man had not been deceived, but had sinned with his eyes open! However, because men I had revered had taught it, I believed it absolutely.

Chapter 13

Another friend came to visit one evening and sat on the floor in my flat. We had spent hours talking back and forth. I was sharing about Jesus and how he could cleanse her from sin, save her soul and give her eternal life, while she was trying to draw me back into my old life. We had argued for such a long time that both of us had run out of words to say.

We sat across the room just staring at each other. I was silently praying, "Lord, help me, I can't get through to my friend. You'll have to help me." Right then, I could feel the Lord enter the room. It was pervading and perceptible. My friend's eyes began to widen. "What did you put in my coffee?" Her voice was low and she looked panicked.

"Nothing. Why?"

"Well, what's this weird feeling?"

"Oh, I didn't realize you could sense him here too!" I had imagined that this was something only I could feel as a comfort from my prayer.

"Wait a minute ... maybe there's a draught coming from under this door." She swivelled around and realized the door was an internal door and there was no breeze.

"Come on now! What's in this coffee?" She was grinning a bit sheepishly.

"This, Helen, is Jesus! This is what I've been telling you about all these hours and you haven't been listening!" She looked at me and squinted suspiciously.

"Tell me, is this a good feeling or an 'out of it feeling'?" I challenged.

She shrugged her shoulders, more in a gesture of trying to

see if she could shake the feeling off. "It's a good feeling. What is it?"

"I just told you, it's God. It is Jesus!"

"He's right here in this room?" It was more of a rhetorical question.

Once she was confident that I was right, that God had literally invaded my funny little home, she said, "Well, what does he want?" And now we had a conversation that was easy. She was left with no choice but to ask Jesus to come into her life. We talked until the early hours of the morning and it was so exciting for me. As I read passages from the Bible to her, she was startled to find that the book was alive. The writer was present with us and it was as if he was speaking to us from the printed page.

Now I had two friends from my old life who needed to grow as believers. They found church odd. So many "straights". They didn't think they could measure up. I tried to help them see that these "straights" had come from all sorts of messed up, broken up, dried up lives themselves. Helen came to church, just to get another "buzz". I kept trying to explain. "You don't just follow Jesus for the 'buzz'. You learn of him, you follow him. He is now your rightful Lord and master."

"Yeah right. So when do I start feeling the 'buzz' again?"

Somehow these new babies were not easy. I took them to the home group. Here, people tried to help me and they were getting used to the collection of characters that came along with me. There was Thaddeus, a skinny, wiry old man who lived around the corner and who opened his home to any drinking buddies. He had befriended Hydra and so I had been introduced to him. Thad would sit in the corner almost under a big wicker basket, his legs pulled up and held by his scrawny arms and his face scowling. But he listened.

I needed help to disciple these two old friends. I had expectations that more of my friends would follow but felt ill-equipped to look after them. For one thing they were too close to my own past life. I was still clawing my own way back to following Jesus. I wondered how I could keep going while carrying others out of the pit with all their weights and mangled lives.

Down the hill there was a Christian community, in a big, old brick mansion. They were expert at helping people and rehabilitating them, but the complex was in its last phases and those working there were tired and ready to move on. However, they had been very encouraging to me. I had simply walked in one day, introduced myself and proceeded to "hang about" for my own growth and strength.

The central leaders of this inner city mission were an American couple. The wife was interested in what was happening with my old friends and was willing to help me.

"You know, I've had a dream from the Lord that something like this should happen. I'd really like to host your group and help you disciple them. But, there's just one thing I'd like you to do."

"Sure."

"It's important that your church backs you and that you are accountable to them."

I was happy with this and couldn't see any reason why they would not agree to my running a small Bible study group, with the support of this well-known ministry. I took the idea to our home group leader to ask on my behalf. So, it was with dismay and confusion that I heard they had not given their approval.

My friends were running out of time. I couldn't hold them much longer but I tried to get them to the official teaching nights and whatever was on the official church programme. They just had so many questions and the "Christianese" and the culture was too foreign.

I took Hydra one night to visit Lottie. Again, I was amazed at God's ability to change a person. We sat in her lovely lounge and Hydra said, "I'd like to come to the church services, but I don't have the clothes! This is about all I've got." She exhibited her black jersey, black jeans, worn old shoes and the floppy old bag covered in embroidered patterns that were so stained that it was hard to distinguish the colours.

"Oh phooey!" dismissed Lottie waving her arms in the air. "What does it matter what you wear to church? God looks on the heart, not the outside! Hey, look at me, I'm an old woman and I feel the cold in my feet, so I wear these 'huggie' boots and no one is going to tell me I can't wear these to church!" She jutted out her jaw in a unique Lottie way and waggled her finger in the air. "God isn't interested in your clothes; he's interested in you!"

Remembering my earlier scrapes with Lottie over the clothes issue, I fought back prickly tears.

One Saturday morning Hydra and Helen arrived at my flat with a loaf of bread.

"Hey! We brought you some bread!"

"Well, thanks."

"No, eat it!"

"I'm not hungry, thanks. I've already had a potato for breakfast."

"Eat the bread. We brought it, eat a piece!"

It seemed stupid and they were so insistent, so I ate a piece of their bread. They both watched me intently.

"What's the problem?" I asked.

"We thought you might be sick."

"Why?"

"Well, we stole the bread."

"So?"

"Well, you are so pure and perfect and into this God stuff so much we thought you might chuck up or die or something."

What was a little stolen bread to what Christ had covered by grace already in my life! I was angry at their stupidity and told them that they had gone back to their sin as a dog goes back to its vomit.[11]

So I began to realize things were slipping a bit with my "babies".

"Walking with Jesus was never meant to be easy. It is a narrow way. You have to make a daily commitment to follow him. It's worth it!"

"Well, it's easy for you! You know what to do," they wailed. I knew they were right in so many ways. I had known Jesus and had a background of Christian understanding. They were so raw and so demonized and I couldn't help them because I was a woman.

They planned to be baptised but on the day they were waylaid by another old friend who took them to the pub, and that was that. I saw them both a few times after this, but they drifted away. It was as if I had been standing in a swift flowing, filthy river trying to hold my friends from being taken by the current. On the shore there were hundreds of people busy organizing a church picnic and even though I called out to them to help, I found that they were too busy. I was weak from having battled the river to get onto the more solid bank but in the end I lost my two friends and had to watch them moving further and further from safety. I have prayed for both of them, along with so many of my other old friends ever since.

I can't condemn my old friends, because I lived with them, knew their scars and their dark torments. I can't feel angry that they are trapped in sin, unless that anger is toward the devil who keeps them slaves. I would love nothing more than to see my old friends come to know Jesus, as I have come to know him.

I was being kept busy in this new life. I was meeting other Christians, socializing with Dinah and Martha and talking with Thad when he dropped in to talk about Jesus.

I had one other social outlet at the time. An advertisement in a local paper had leapt off the page at me. I knew it was one of those moments where God was highlighting something to me and this advert began to plague me. He wanted me to go to a club called ITC and learn public speaking! This was terrifying to me. I couldn't speak publicly even for a few seconds without my mind going totally blank. The mere thought of joining this club terrified me, especially since I couldn't go with the help of drink.

In blind obedience I had gone to a meeting. It had been newly formed in Ponsonby, a nearby inner city suburb. There was a small group of mostly older ladies and they were so encouraging and kind. The first opening "thought" I had to bring to the club meeting only had to be one sentence. It had me quivering and awake the whole night beforehand. I got through it with much trembling.

This group started to draw me out. Soon I had given a few very short speeches and the training they gave was helping my "butterflies fly in formation", as they had promised it would do. I could never have imagined that in years to come my occupation would be as a minister and an itinerant preacher who found it difficult to keep messages as short as possible!

In these early days my Christian friends were wary of me. I didn't quite fit any particular mould. Karen came to visit me one morning and found me lying on the floor rubbing my stomach.

"What's wrong?" she said, quite worried.

"Oh, nothing, it's just some of the potatoes for breakfast were green and when that happens, it takes a bit for the tummy pains to go away. I'll be fine."

I still remember the strange look on her face. I knew potatoes for breakfast wasn't quite the same as cornflakes, but when all I could afford was a bag of potatoes, this was breakfast, lunch and dinner and toward the end of the bag sometimes the pickings were slim.

Geoff tried to match me with some of the young single

women in the church. One left after sitting on my camp stretcher on the pile of curtains and looking a bit bewildered. One, Molly, managed to retain some form of friendship, but I could tell she thought I was very weird. She told me so quite often.

Jesus was my constant companion and my relationship with him was becoming so wonderful, I wasn't very interested in fostering too many other relationships anyway. At last I had found love and I wasn't keen to share the time I set aside for him.

The Bible was speaking to me. One day I was reading from Jeremiah and the words at the start of the book jumped off the page at me: "I knew you from the womb, I have appointed you as a prophet to the nations."[12] I wondered what it meant. Then with a horror, I knew God was calling me to do some work for him. I was only just capable of a five-minute speech at ITC and dreading it. How could he ask me to do something like speak to groups of people?

I phoned my sister and she said, "Oh yes. God told me this was your destiny years ago! I've never told you because it was something you had to hear for yourself. The Lord told me that my ministry was to pray for you. But the way the Lord brings this about in your life may be far different from what you think."

I was dumbfounded. Did God ever keep any secrets from my sister? No wonder she had prayed for me all through my rebellious, broken years. She was going to have to exercise a lot more faith now, if this inner city derelict was ever to be used in such a way. But then God does choose the foolish things of this world.[13]

He began to teach me about the responsibility and the reality of ministry and speaking as an emissary for God. This was the cause of serious contemplation and there was much Jesus taught me over this time.

About three months after I had been attending the mid-week meeting, spring was starting and I was happily enjoying a clear, alcohol-free, marijuana-free, relationship-free life. I loved to get to the home group each week. I loved every person there, from the dear old ladies to the funny and weird crazies. They were just my family.

I thought about my old friends and how that around this time, couples often came out of their winter hibernation, unhappy with their partners. The nights were getting longer and spring seemed to bring out new hope of clubbing, romancing and often a change in lovers. This spring, at last, I was free from the dance, free from the pressure to find that perfect soulmate or hold onto the one I thought I had found.

About then, a young man came to the group. He was 22 and from his shaved haircut I could tell he was fresh from the punk scene. He looked such a youthful young fellow with blue eyes and a tidy, striped top over white shorts. I thought to myself, "Hmm, nice young fellow. Way too young for me to even consider even if I had an interest. I wonder who I can match-make him onto?"

He was looking over at me and thinking, "Hmm, little miss church girl. Been nowhere, done nothing. Quite nice though."

I chatted with this new addition over coffee and discovered he had been a drummer in punk bands and had been a Christian about two months. He had become a Christian about the same time that I came back to the Lord. I told him just a little of my story and he listened attentively. His name was Peter.

Chapter 14

My lack of work was worrying me considerably; I was having a hard time trying to get more than a few days here and there. November was just upon me. The week I met Peter, I received a call from the editor of a trade magazine that I wrote for. I had been writing a satirical column for some time and the editor, who was a friend of mine, had been keen for me to write some features.

"What are you doing next week?"

"Well, nothing. I don't have any work."

"Good. How would you like to go to Tahiti and cover an inaugural cruise around the Tahitian islands?"

"Yeah..." I was a little concerned because even though the trip would be paid for, I would still have expenses and I couldn't pack a bag of "spuds" to keep myself fed.

"The airfares and accommodation and the cruise will all be paid for. The cruise is all-inclusive. The only thing is that you'll have to go up five days earlier than the cruise to fit in with flights. You'll be staying at a lovely beach hotel. The only costs you'll have will be for meals over these five days. Your passport's up to date, isn't it?"

"Yes." I was still a travel agent.

"All you would have to do is write us an article for the magazine when you get back. What do you say?"

I had a new boss in my life. "I'll let you know."

"OK, but I'd like you to go."

Once off the phone, I prayed. "Lord, if this is something you want me to do, then let me know. But if it is, I'll need a little money. I'll need a few hundred and I have no idea where it will come from. But, if this is in your will, you can provide it." The next day, Dot phoned me from her home on Waiheke Island.

"Hey. You know how you left your old VW car over here?"

"Yeah. I don't know what to do about it. It isn't going, is it?"

"Nope. But I might be able to solve your problem. I have a buyer and I think you are going to like this, since you are a God person now. It's a Christian guy and his name is Hope! He says he'll give you $400 for it."

"Wow! Sell the car."

I had my spending money. Now God had my attention. I was convinced that he was about to send me on some important mission, just as I had dreamed as a child, God's secret agent! After all, if he had gone to this much trouble and expense, it must be for a purpose, not to mention how he had been speaking to me about ministry! I phoned the editor and said I'd go.

The flight was to depart late on Thursday night, so I was able to pack and go to the home group first before flying out. I was dressed my best in my only good skirt and top, ready for the tropics. Being paid for by an airline meant honouring that privilege by dressing appropriately.

A new girl was at the home group, a hippie born out of her time. This was the 80s not the 70s but she had come along as a friend of Peter's. We talked in the coffee time after the meeting. I was sitting on the floor in my good clothes. She looked at me with a wondering expression and said, "Wow, so, what's it like to be so straight? I mean, I could never be straight like you! I mean, wow, like, look at your clothes! I'm sorry, I don't mean to be rude, it's just, hey wow, I just can't imagine what it must be like to be straight like you."

No one had called me "straight", ever. I was an original hippie, then a lesbian. I couldn't answer her. I just laughed. This new life was full of surprises and far more interesting encounters with people than I could have imagined.

I was so pumped up with expectation and confidence of God's purpose as I set out on the flight. Jesus and I were going to Tahiti. Then an odd thing happened. Up until now, for weeks, I had felt the constant, unmistakable presence of Jesus with me. But as I walked down the gangway and stepped onto Tahitian soil, that sense dissipated. I was alone.

I tried to rationalize. Feelings are so subjective. I was tired. Feelings meant nothing. I had no doubt God wanted me here and that was enough. I found my hotel and stepped into a light and pleasant room overlooking the garden. There was just one painting on the wall: it was a depiction of Eve and the snake.

"I bind the power in that painting," I muttered religiously and settled into the room.

My money wasn't going to last forever and I was well aware of how this could be fast spent on cold drinks in this hot climate. I was busy the first day, bouncing into town on "le Bus", a rough truck with wooden benches in the back. I stocked up on supermarket soft drinks and anything I could take back to snack on as replacements for my potatoes. There was no way I could afford meals in the hotel.

It was a bit lonely in paradise. I could swim in the pool, walk the beach, visit the town and inspect other hotels, since the travel agent in me had to be satisfied. I spent a lot of time in my room, praying and pondering the painting. Jesus didn't feel so close. His book was dry.

On the other hand God was dealing with me in a very clear way. Now that I had repented and returned to my faith, I wondered how the Lord would guide me. For all the years I had been living my crazy lifestyle, I had hidden in my heart an ongoing admiration for Greg. When I had been unable to pray for myself at the depths of my misery, I would sometimes remember him and pray for him. It had been an odd love. I would never know if he had ever had feelings for me and this had haunted me in a way that had caused me to make an idol of him. He had gone on following Jesus, had married and perhaps had children now. He was in ministry and as far as I knew, successful.

In my deepest, secret self, I had wondered if God might somehow take his wife so that I could, by a miracle, still marry Greg. It was a stupid thought but it plagued me. Not that I wished his wife dead. I didn't know her and in some ways I saw her as someone who had won Greg's heart and therefore was obviously better than me. I could never have competed with her, so I had no malice toward her personally.

Here in Tahiti, I was strongly aware that by walking away from the will of God, I had forfeited Greg. It was time to let go and let that old dream die. On the other hand, I was so grateful I had found my way home to a relationship with God again. I began to give God thanks for this, singing and praising in my hotel room. Then I heard in my heart, as loudly as I might have heard someone speak, "I brought you back not just for your own good, but for my purposes!"

I was pulled up short in my rejoicing and with a sense of humiliation, realized that this was not about "me" but about HIM. It had more to do with God's plans and the work he had for me, than my personal preservation. Yes, he wanted the best for me, but I had wasted God's valuable time by messing about, living away from him and now I was keenly aware of my responsibility.

Like my bus-driver friend and her vision of being rescued from that dark place, I knew now how it must have felt to have been dragged from the pit by the hand of a captain. Now it was as if my face was being drawn to him and in his eyes were those same tears, but this time they were for me.

I thought about phoning the French Assemblies of God church. I had already discovered where this was in the town. Sitting on my bed I would go over the phrases of French to try to have a conversation with whoever would answer the phone. My schoolgirl French was rusty and the phrase book I had brought was full of useless phrases such as, "How often does it snow here?" I gave up the thought and set about trying to fill in my five days.

I spent some of my precious funds and took a day tour around the island. I had been keen to see the Paul Gaugin museum and wasn't disappointed. The gardens were serene and restful, complete with water lilies and flora almost like living illustrations of the original paintings. This painter had immortalized the verdant plant life, along with the human colour and sensual warmth of these islands on canvas. I could feel the pull of temptation as if I were Eve wandering in Eden.

On Sunday I visited the Assemblies of God church. It was a low square tropical building, painted in the popular, dusty yellow in which all such buildings seem to be painted. The interior was humble and furnished with an assortment of old chairs, a table at the front and a dark wooden cross on the wall.

As I entered I was met by the pastor's wife.

"Bonjour," she said.

"Bonjour," I replied. "I'm visiting from New Zealand."

"Oh! You speak English!" The strong American accent came back. The church was being looked after temporarily by an American couple. I told her that I had wanted to phone the church but had been lacking confidence in my French. She said this was humbling to her as she had just this week decided that she would stop answering her phone as her French was so inadequate and she was embarrassed when people phoned. She was going to let her husband answer if he were home but now she realized she would have ignored my call if I had phoned and she felt compelled to keep trying.

I explained what I was doing and how God had brought me to the islands. I was a little doubtful now about why I was there, but still had some hope for the cruise time.

The pastor's wife said to her husband, "Darling, we need to pray for this young girl. Going out on that cruise will not be easy as these islands have strong seductive spirits." Later I was glad of her wisdom and grateful for their prayers, though I had no chance to ever thank this couple as the return of the cruise was tightly matched to my return flight.

The next day, as my money was running out, I received my first invitation to a dinner. It was the night before the cruise and the dinner was in the hotel where I was staying. I learned that the group had been dining in different places every day and I had missed every invitation but this one. I could have done with the free meals, but perhaps what I didn't need was the extra time with the group.

No sooner had I arrived in the buffet restaurant but members of the cruise party came up to me, to welcome me with wide smiles and quizzical looks. A tall man with olive skin and dark hair came over to greet me. He had a neat, clipped beard and a handsome, intelligent face. He was wearing a tailored casual suit and had an assured but gentle manner.

"Well, hi!" His dark eyes creased with his relaxed smile. His accent was east coast American. "So, you're the long lost journalist from New Zealand?"

"Yes." I was feeling a little small and like someone who had gatecrashed a party of old friends.

"Come and sit with us." He kindly took my elbow and guided me to his table where a group of middle-aged Americans was engaged in a lively discussion about the islands. They ushered me to the table as if this was my allocated place. The younger man who had met with me told me his name was Nicholas Levi. He accompanied me to the buffet, where we exchanged our names and I explained that I was really quite a fledgling writer. I wanted to get things straight from the start. This was my first travel feature.

These professionals could have made me nervous if I had

tried to pretend to be in their league. Nicholas was the managing editor of a travel magazine based in New York, but worldwide in circulation. His travels had taken him far and wide. My own travel agent trips had been pretty sparse to date and at this stage I hadn't yet made Europe. This was one of many cruises he had covered, but he was careful not to sound boastful. He somehow turned his interest to me and appeared not to be very impressed with his own skills or experience.

I went to bed feeling that the cruise tomorrow would be a new beginning in whatever it was that the Lord had brought me to Tahiti to do. I blamed the devil for having kept me from the group and looked forward to finding a candidate to share my faith with. Now that I had met some of the group, I could board and know there were friends already there.

I bid *adieu* to the painting of Eve's temptation. I could escape this harbinger of potential sin, but had completely missed its warning. The other passengers were either travel writers, directors of large wholesale travel companies from the USA, or French journalists, French movie stars and local celebrities from Tahiti.

I had learned long before that the best thing to do was to buy very plain clothes that mixed and matched. Woolworths provided white trousers and a striped white and red top. This felt nautical enough to wear on board for my first day and supplemented my second-hand ensembles.

The ship held around 70 passengers so was quite intimate. It was freshly painted and sat on the water like an innocent white bride awaiting her honeymoon. There was a lounge and dining room on one deck. Every room was an outside room with a porthole to watch the new island destinations growing larger as the ship came to each one.

I was led to my room, which was like a small hotel room, complete with a bathroom. I wondered how I would be on this cruise. I had tried to forget that I had been horribly seasick once when I was thirteen and had taken an overnight sea trip from Wellington to Lyttleton in the South Island on an old inter-island ferryboat called the Wahine.

I had been glad the trip had not been a few months later as this ship foundered in the Wellington harbour and many lives had been lost. As we had watched the black and white TV pictures on the news, I had empathized with the passengers who had perished in the ice cold waters. I would not have had the strength to save myself after the night of seasickness that had started before we had ever left the harbour.

The first obligation was to appear on deck and assemble to hear the ship's safety drill. This was a flat-bottomed boat, designed to cruise rivers, where it had been working up until now, or to sail into the lagoons of tropical islands where a deeper hulled boat would not be able to navigate. It was not an ocean-going boat, though it had been sailed down from the west coast of the USA and had proved to be as seaworthy as any other small cruise ship.

We sat about on canvas chairs, me in the one selected by Nicholas, listening to a crew member take us through the lifeboat drill. The ship's crew had drawn in the ropes and we were slowly moving across the lagoon of Papeete with the stunning peaks of the mountains of Moorea just ahead of us, a mere 30 minutes away.

A few minutes after leaving the wharf we set out over the reef and into the ocean. Already the new island had drawn closer. The ship began to rise and fall with the higher waves and rolled from one side to the other. I started to lose what the speaker was saying. I was feeling the effect of the seasickness pills I had taken. Perhaps I had taken a dosage that was too strong? It was as if fever was welling in my head and my stomach began to lurch. I just had enough time to return to my room before I was wretchedly sick.

Nicholas had watched as the colour drained to white in

my face and had jumped to my weak request to be excused and walked me to my cabin.

"Are you sure you don't want me to stay?"

"No, I'll be fine. I'll just lie down for a bit, might be the seasickness pills ... " I was eager to be left alone; there was nothing dignified about vomiting. I lay on the bed, trying to imagine the next five days. Soon the rolling and pitching died and the ship remained steady. We had crossed into the aqua lagoon of Moorea.

I recovered quickly and chided myself on the double dose I had gulped down, convincing myself that one pill would do the trick next time. My new group of friends welcomed me as I returned to the deck and my cheeks were again a healthy peach pink. The island before me drew me with its magic. I had already forgotten my bed; the day was just starting and the sky above was blue, but pale compared to the vibrant blues of the sea.

We docked and were taken by bus to a resort for lunch. It was a collection of low buildings nestled into a bay with a sweep of coconut palms and hibiscus bushes alive with red, orange or yellow delicate flowers that splashed Gaugin's tropical colour over the seascape. A crescent of white sand was lapped by crystal water as warm as a thermal pool.

After lunch we lounged about watching the sea breaking white and thin, far away on the distant rim of the reef. Talk was of comparisons of tropical fish and the best places to snorkel in the world. Most had enjoyed the Caribbean and enthused about the colours of the fish, the clarity of the water, but my first love was Fiji. There, the marine reserves meant a sea teeming with rainbow fish and forests of coloured coral and I could reach these wonderlands just a few metres from the shore of my resort island.

The Americans were fascinated as none had visited the Fijian islands and they bombarded me with questions. It seemed wrong for me to boast of my opinions when they had experienced the Caribbean, the Indian Ocean and the Mediterranean, and all I had known so far was Fiji. Nicholas listened; by now he was always at my side. He was in his mid-thirties and I was starting to enjoy his sense of humour and quick and agile mind.

The resort had a long wooden pier and Nicholas and I decided to go snorkelling. No one else wanted to join us so we enjoyed the quiet underwater world together. The surprises of the sea always delighted me and I was pleased there was some-one to enjoy one of my favourite pursuits with me. Floating with our masks under the surface we drifted about like two sea turtles, slowly moving across the water, sometimes waving or patting the other's arm to point out some exceptional sight, a bright yellow angel fish or a chalk blue starfish settled on white soft sand. The afternoon was one of those "forever" afternoons.

Later we sat on the canvas lounge chairs on the sand with another couple. Every one was topless and because this had never been a problem for me in the past, it didn't seem to be a problem to me then either. It was French territory and would have seemed almost peculiar to not be topless. It had been days since I had felt the closeness of Jesus and I hadn't thought to ask him if this was acceptable. Besides, I had already made my pact that unless God loudly said "No", I refused to make this new life with him legalistic.

Nicholas sat next to me and we talked about interview techniques for journalists. He suggested that I interview one of the owners of the ship to get some quotes for my story. He taught me how to go about this and then I practised some of these new techniques by interviewing one of the Americans in our group, who was sitting on the other side of me in this beach setting. I perched on my lounge chair with a notepad and a pen, wearing only my bikini pants, and interviewed the American executive.

I loved to be free. I loved the feeling of warm tropical air and the aroma of coconut oil and frangipani and gardenia flowers wafting in the atmosphere. Everything about these islands was sensuous, just as my life before had been. This was paradise for lovers and I had so much to learn about boundaries.

We dropped anchor in the celebrated, picturesque Cook's Bay. The volcanic crags loomed above in silhouette across a lagoon of deepening green. Lights along the shore where small homes dotted the road around the island necklaced the dark scoop of the land. The wine was French and excellent during dinner as we ate at long tables. I was now established with the American party; Nicholas sat across from me and I was comfortable with him.

Nicholas would take my arm with a protective and considerate care. He knew how to make me laugh and we had begun to have our own known cues as we discovered these islands with our combined observations. I was already praying for him as I wanted to keep the Lord foremost in my mind and surely this was the reason for our quick compatibility?

The next day, we cruised to Raiatea. Palm-fringed bays and houses could be seen dotted sparsely in amongst the trees. I had to get the conversation onto my faith. I had already explained that I was a Christian and this had not fazed Nicholas at all. He had good friends who were Christians and the scriptures were a subject of strong interest. He was part Jewish.

We talked of the Bible but he stumbled at the thought of a personal relationship with Jesus. It must only be a matter of time before I would win him. In the meantime, I should be careful. Not that I had any stirring of desire. The thought of a romance with a man was still a mystery to me. Yet, Nicholas was fast becoming a warm friend and we had so much in common. I admired his intelligent conversation and, in his own way, he was tall, dark and handsome. His eyes were always on me.

This attention mystified me as I could see he had made me his target from the first day we met. I looked about on the cruise and had to admit that there were not too many other English-speaking, single, young women on board. But there were other potentials and, of the pickings, I was probably closer to the bottom of the range. I was young, still in reasonable shape from years of disco dancing but hardly a beauty queen and short at 5ft 2 inches.

My face was not unattractive but I had always seen my unruly hair as my nemesis. Sometimes it bounced into natural masses of soft brown curls, but at other times it was a mass of candyfloss tossed anywhere it wanted to settle. Nicholas remarked that he loved my naturalness and that I presented myself in a fresh and unpretentious way.

So far the Woolworths ensemble had worked. Charity shops provided the bulk of my evening wear and day creations. So it was with some secret amusement that I thanked my American women friends as they exclaimed, "Oh, Shirley! You have the loveliest clothes! I just wish we could get such beautiful designs back home!" The famous emperor came to mind as I shrugged and said, "Oh well, we do have some great boutiques."

On Raiatea we went to a village to watch some local dancers. Something about island drums lures me and as I watched the girls interpreting the wild passion of the beat, I worked hard not to watch their lithe bodies or to think of anything other than the art. I began to forgive the missionaries of Tahiti who had lived through hundreds of these nights, with the backdrop curtain of a flame-red evening sky turning day into sensual, tropical night, and who had so often failed in their struggles against temptation.

The nights fell quickly after the sunsets and in the dusk of the evening I knew I had little time before I would have to go back to my room to wait out the long and heaving night.

"Come on," invited Nicholas, "let's go to the bow of the boat. Come and see what happens as we get out to sea."

"I don't know, Nicholas, I'll probably have to pike out as soon as we get beyond the reef."

"Come on. I want to show you."

We went into the most forward lounge. No one else was there and as the sea swelled into looming sheets of water it washed over the window and waves became walls of the deep and salty wash. Nicholas was exhilarated. I began to feel queasy.

"It's time for Cinderella to get home before I am embarrassed by my inevitable reactions!"

Nicholas looked at me with deep sympathy and walked me back to my cabin.

"I'm sorry," I mumbled as I retreated as quickly as I could. "Good night."

"Thanks for showing me the bow. It was scary."

Nicholas laughed. With his eyes he asked, "Do you want me to stay with you?"

My reply was a smile. "Good night, Nicholas, I'll see you tomorrow when I am human again."

At least, I comforted myself, it was keeping Nicholas at bay. I didn't want to have to offend him, but I had no intention of taking this relationship any further.

The morning sun revealed a long lagoon with small islands, the inner motus (islands) of Huahine. We were to have a picnic lunch on one of these. I hoped it would be a motu like those I could see that were perfect rounds of green, like puddings centred in a vanilla custard, palm trees bending sometimes parallel with the sand and others waving slightly in a high breeze.

At breakfast one of the American women wanted to help me.

"These are great. They really work. They have a slow release and will keep you from feeling any seasickness at all. Try them." She handed me some little plasters to stick on my skin.

I would try anything. My seasickness pills weren't working. I gratefully stuck the plaster on. From here on, the seasickness was vanquished.

We moored at a very basic port. Standing on the deck we watched as a local dance team came to welcome us. They were singing and swaying in rows along the dock. The girls wore tourist yellow grass skirts and bikini tops made of varnished coconut shells, tied with string. I winced, thinking of fitting the right cup sizes and how uncomfortable they must be!

I felt like royalty as I disembarked and was garlanded with strings of exquisitely perfumed flowers, tiare, frangipani and gardenias. The heady perfumes enveloped my senses and it seemed that the whole village had come to greet us. The French TV stars were most in demand and there was a cacophony of laughter and talk and arms flinging in embrace and singing and dancing. I laughed just to be in the midst of this scene.

Nicholas rushed up to my side. "Come on, quickly, Marie has organized a trip into the inland to visit her parents and she has invited a few to go with her!"

I ran with Nicholas, wondering about this spontaneous diversion from the boat, but as eager as he was to experience more local colour. He tugged me up onto the "bus" truck and it lurched out across a dirt road.

Marie originated from this island and she was Chinese-Tahitian. She spoke Mandarin, Tahitian and English well. I had no idea what her part on the cruise was all about but she was elated to have this chance to visit her parents. On the truck there was a small group gathered including some friends of Marie's.

"How do we get back to the ship?" I wondered.

"No problem," Nicholas assured me. "We'll meet with the ship on the other side of the island as it's mooring over there later today."

As the truck rumbled on its way, I wondered whether this had been properly organized. After some time bumping over local roads, we were deposited outside a tropical store. A faded old Coca-Cola sign was fixed to the wall that may have had paint in an earlier era. The store opening was a dark door in the side of this shed-like building. Washing was drooping from a wire clothesline to the side of the store and all around was the lush vegetation of the inland. Huge-leafed plants elbowed for room with wide spear-like palm leaves; bushes and hibiscus shrubs thrust out their arms adorned with pastel pink and outrageous red and orange clusters of flowers.

Marie disappeared into the store, which was also her family home. She reappeared with a small, slightly bent man, his face sun-leathered and creased with smiles. "My father!" she introduced happily. We smiled and "*Bonjoured*" and nodded to other family members and dogs and anyone who sauntered past to see this odd assortment of Americans and Tahitian celebrities.

Watermelon, sliced and piled in giant wedges, appeared on plates. We gratefully gorged on these grinning curves of sweet, dripping fruit. My photo ended up in the Tahiti Press, snapped as I wrapped a slice of watermelon around my face.

Caught in a carefree morning of laughter and watermelon, I looked at Nicholas who was watching me with amusement lighting his dark eyes as we hitch-hiked back to the ship. We felt as if we shared a secret like naughty schoolchildren who had escaped a school picnic to discover a hidden waterfall.

Arriving back at our boat, we found it moored in a crescent bay of beauty, now anticipated but still a delight. Our captain was not amused. Marie received a few heated words and we slunk away hoping not to be reprimand further. The air cleared within minutes.

In front of the resort, the flawless, soft sea-carpet could be seen in a wide arch through crystal water. It was impossible for Nicholas and me not to be tempted to a swim. By now it felt like I had known Nicholas forever and nothing of my life in New Zealand existed.

At night a local dance troupe entertained us as the sun surrendered in fire streaks of black cloud and flames of yellow that lit the sky and turned the palm trees into silhouettes. Wine flowed and I was careful to stay with one glass, now that I had the freedom to do so. The drums throbbed and oiled warriors danced, flexing their muscles in wild, sexual innuendo behind the girls, as they flicked their skirts at impossible speed. Nicholas gathered me to him with an affectionate embrace of his arm.

I excused myself once dark came and we were heading out of the lagoon. I wasn't sure how the new cure would work and didn't want to risk any queasiness. In confusion of mind, I wanted to read my Bible and talk to the silent Lord, who must surely still be with me. His word promised it. Why was it he now felt so remote?

The masterpiece of the master painter greeted us in the new day in Bora Bora. By now, faint traces of floral perfumes were drifting from the land to soak the senses and entice us to the shores. The spirits of Bora Bora beckoned with coconut branches spreading their welcoming flags. "Come to the islands of love," the winds breathed. "Abandon your worries. We know nothing but languid nights of love."

I walked on my own through the day, wearing a crown of flowers on my head and garlands draped over my island wrap-around cover.

"Where did you go?" Nicholas chided quizzically.

"Just walking."

In the evening we visited a resort to dance at the night-club. The night pulsated with island music and the vibration of feet. There were just a few of us from the boat on shore and when it came time to return, we walked a lane of moonlit tropical gardens. Nicholas and I held hands as we wandered silently back to the ship.

This was wrong and I felt no attraction for Nicholas other than the closeness of these few days that now seemed a life-time in paradise. I would have to explain to him that this romance was confusing me. He was not a Christian and I couldn't see God's plan in bringing us together. He was closed to anything other than intellectual assent to the scriptures. My lesbian lifestyle was too close behind and it all felt wrong. I couldn't summon any genuine feeling for this person, as it was too weird, his being male.

Our journey was fast ending; this would be our last night on board. The long journey back overnight would bring us back to Papeete and my last night at the hotel before an early morning flight home. The cloud drifted in shreds across the full moon, as we stood on the deck alone.

Nicholas took me in his arms and kissed me gently.

"Nicholas," I stumbled. "I don't know that I want to go down this path."

"I want you to come back to New York with me. You can write for the magazine."

"I mean ... it's just ... "

"That you are a Christian? It's OK, I respect that."

"Yes, but it's a bit more than that." I sighed. "Well, at least part of it is that I am a bit confused about all this. You see, up until I came back to Jesus I had been living as a lesbian ... I'm just not attracted to men."

"I understand. I've been bisexual myself and understand

fully. You don't have to feel uncomfortable with me. I know where you are coming from."

"But..."

He kissed me again and we stood in this perfect shipboard romantic setting with just the faintest zephyr of a warm breath of heady island breeze. My mind raced. He would certainly ask me to his room. I didn't feel compelled but in the past I had never been able to say no for fear of offending or hurting a person's feelings. My own had never counted.

"I've got something I want to give you."

"Oh, I'm not sure..."

"Hey, I'm not trying to pressure you. Honest. It's in my cabin, come with me." He watched my face and could read my apprehension. "I want you to stay with me tonight."

"I... I can't, Nicholas." I had done it! Said "No". "My faith means more to me now than anything. I can't just throw it away again."

"OK." He opened his hands and smiled at me. "No pressure. It's OK. But I do have something for you. It's your birthday the day after tomorrow isn't it?"

"Wow! How did you remember that? Even I have forgotten! After all, I am going to lose it on the flight over the dateline!" I laughed.

"Come on." He led me to the second deck where he opened his cabin. I stood awkwardly at the door. He reappeared with a colourful printed muslin wraparound.

"Happy birthday," he whispered. "I bought this for you when we were in Moorea."

"It's lovely, but I can't..."

"Stay with me. Just tonight."

"I can't." My resolve was weakening but only because I hated to disappoint. "I can't..." I ended weakly, throwing a prayer to the silent listener.

"It's OK." He bent and kissed me again and we walked

back to my cabin. I was a bit dumbstruck. I had won. I had done it. I was back safe in my cabin. I could have had a ticket to New York to live with a successful, tall dark and handsome, intelligent man, working as a writer. My dreams had been offered like royal dainty morsels[14] and I had refused the feast.

At the dock we were packed and dressed for our homeward journeys. Nicholas smiled and put his arms around me.

"Goodbye. I hope somehow we might meet again."

"Me too," I said, genuinely.

He climbed aboard a bus taking the Americans back to the airport. Their flight would go in a few short hours. Nicholas was dressed in a slate grey business suit.

The bus for my hotel growled onto the dock and I climbed aboard, finding a seat where I could see Nicholas in his bus. He waved and we both grinned. Then his bus turned and rolled toward the airport. My own bus was not far behind. The route took us via the airport, driving past the travellers standing about waiting for luggage to be uplifted.

I thought I had seen Nicholas for the last time at the dock but there he was. His suit looked darker in the shadow of the building. He didn't see me as we slowly passed the buildings. He was wearing dark sunglasses and as he half turned, his face, shadowed and expressionless, was somehow foreign to me and cold. I shuddered as if a sinister shroud had fallen about this man that I had known for just six days.

Alone and waiting for the flight in the early hours of the morning, I couldn't sleep. I didn't trust this hotel that had so often missed sending me messages. How could I be sure I would get the wake up call? But I was also in confusion. I felt somehow that I had failed God. No one had come to know Jesus through my journey and I had come so close to personal failure.

Soon I was speeding to the airport. Flying home the hours went by, then we hit the dateline and I suddenly lost my birthday along with another day. Perhaps I could say I had never turned 29, since the day had been stolen? I was more concerned about coming back to New Zealand, now that it was close to Christmas and I had no known work ahead of me.

Chapter 15

My tan, if that was what I could call the insignificant colour on my white skin, was already fading. However, the obsession for a job was growing. I had been plaguing the temp agencies that I was registered with but it was getting close to Christmas and few places would take on a worker this close to statutory holidays. I had walked the length of the city checking which stores were busy and offering temporary help whenever I saw a harassed retailer.

The home group had just finished praying for any needs and we had begun to chat. I looked across at the young ex-punk, Peter. As I did, I heard my voice say, "How's that woman at your work that we prayed for a couple of weeks ago?"

Peter looked startled. I felt the same way, as I couldn't remember even praying for a woman at his work.

"What woman?"

I was hoping he wouldn't ask. Then his eyes looked for a second to the ceiling and he said, "Oh, yeah, I remember, we prayed for her but she's left now. She frew the job in." I noticed Peter mixed his f's and th's.

"Oh?" I said hopefully. "Then maybe you need someone temporary at your work?" I had a job waiting for me after Christmas in a travel agency but it didn't start for four weeks.

"Maybe. I'll ask the boss tomorrow," said Peter.

The next day he phoned me and said, "I checked wif the boss and he said he could do wif someone, but just for free and a half weeks, just to Christmas. He can't give you any work beyond this."

"Just for three and a half weeks!" Perfect! This was exactly the timing I needed! It was a divine set up. I could start right away.

The next day I met Peter on the bus. He looked pleased to see me but a little cagey. He watched with interest as we stopped to pick up passengers at the next stop. The bus ended its journey at the bottom of town and we had to walk to the job. Peter looked back a couple of times as we walked along and I wondered what was distracting him. We fell to talking about our faith and I listened carefully as Peter sometimes stuttered a little and stumbled over his words.

I was assigned a job collating paper and working on a staple machine. The work was carried out in the printer's area. Two huge printing machines clacked and roared while the printer sat by his beloved machines, reading novels. Every now and then he would check something or add ink or watch for opportunities to tease me, or the university student who was working with me. The printer's favourite entertainment, however, was to hurl abuse or taunts at Peter.

My friend and I talked as we worked at our tedious jobs and kept half an eye on the door where the boss might emerge. If he caught us chatting amidst the cacophony of machine noise, he would scream reprimands and insults. We were expected to keep our minds fully on the job, "one sheet, two sheet, three sheet, and click". A young hormone-exploding teenager was commandeered to help us and as he had his back to the crocodile's door, he was the one to be chewed most often.

Nothing irritated me more than the sly, snide goads the printer prodded at Pete. The printer was tall and solid. He enjoyed standing over Pete who was short and slim built. I started to call the printer Goliath. Pete never retaliated, but just got on with his work. More than anything else Goliath loved to ridicule Pete's faith. This was enough for me.

"Hey, Goliath! You enjoy being a low-life, huh?" I snapped at him.

"What's it to you, mouth!" he grunted.

"I guess you feel inferior to Pete do you, Goliath? Is that why you keep trying to push him?"

"Shut up, mouth! Who pushed your button?"

"What Pete is inside is bigger than you, buddy. I'd be careful about who you pick on. You laugh at his God, but one day, Goliath, you'll be flat on your face before him and Pete will still be standing."

He pulled a face and hid behind his book.

"I laugh at you picking on Pete. You're a coward to pick on him just because he's physically smaller than you. You're a flea compared to him on the inside."

He pretended he couldn't hear me over the rattle of the machine. He put his hand to his ear in a dramatic gesture of deafness. But he drew back from his ridicule. Every morning we greeted each other, "Good morning, Goliath."

"Gidday, mouth."

On about the third day that I had been working in the printing business, Pete and I went to eat our lunch in the tiny park that was a wedge of green between two roads. We sat on the grass and talked about Jesus. I had told him a little of my story, particularly about my heavy drinking and how the Lord had dealt with me. He had told me his story about how he had been dumped by his live-in girlfriend and how through this, he had given his life to Jesus.

"Y'know," he confessed, "before you came to work wif me, I'd met a girl on the bus who I sat with each day and she works in the lunchbar, just down from work. I fink she feels a bit put out because I don't sit wif her any more or walk to work wif her."

"Hey! You don't have to sit with me. I don't mind if she walks with us."

"Have you seen her?"

"The one in the lunchbar? Yeah, I think I know the one you mean. She's kind of tiny and pretty."

He munched thoughtfully. "I've been getting to know her."

"Oh yeah."

"Yeah, I'm wanting to get to know her because I'm going to tell her about Jesus soon ... "

At this I fell back onto the grass and laughed out loud. Pete blushed and frowned at me.

"When?" I tried to stop my laughter. "When were you planning to talk to her about Jesus?"

"Well ... I was just waiting for the right time."

"Yeah, right, Peter!"

The next day, we talked again. Peter had thought a lot about it and realized he had been kidding himself.

"Y'know, I had been finking maybe she was going to become a Christian and she might be the right person for me."

"She's a real dolly-bird." I had noticed she was well groomed and wore tasteful make-up.

"She's intelligent, too."

"I wouldn't know." This new Christian was hungry for God and I'd found myself drawing on my earlier Bible College knowledge to help disciple him.

"Just one problem."

"Mmmm?"

"Just the other day, before you started work, she said to me, 'My husband works on fishing boats, and when he's away, I like to play, if you know what I mean ... ' I didn't know she was married, but I'd been tempted. Tempted to throw in my faif. She's everything I'd dreamt of."

"Except that she's already married."

"I didn't know that."

"And not a Christian, but you were planning to work on that, maybe ... "

"Ok, you've had your laugh."

The spell was broken. Peter forgot his lady friend and she stopped catching his bus, even after I was long gone from the job.

Now, added to my "Monopoly" friend and the assortment of Thaddeus and others, Peter visited as well. At least he had no overwhelming problems and was, like me, wanting more than anything else to know God.

Chapter 16

As summer drew on we would bus into town to the Tuesday night Bible teaching sessions. Then walk back through the city, up College Hill to Ponsonby and Peter would accompany me to my flat in Herne Bay before walking back to where he boarded with a young couple a few streets away.

His story to faith began through his love of music. One of Peter's favourite bands was Lynard Skynard. They had a theme song, "I'm a free bird, I'm a free spirit, going along, and God knows I will never change." The song troubled him one night as he listened to it on a radio on his way home with friends. The leader of the band had been killed when the plane the band had been flying in crashed. The band broke up because of the death and the serious injuries of its members. Here was their song saying, "and God knows I will never change", and now the leader was dead and would stand before God. Peter was keenly aware that he was journeying down the same road and he wanted to push away the thought that God had to be faced one way or another.

Some years before, Peter's mother had become a Christian and his grandmother was already a strong believer and a praying woman. His gran had told him about a missionary in her church, an old man that Peter knew. This man, Hayden Mellsop, had been in China and during the Japanese invasion he had been placed before a firing squad. Others before him had just been shot. Then, without any explanation, the soldiers spared his life and he lived to return and tell the story.

This old missionary's sister and a friend had been walking down the road one day while he was away and had suddenly had an urge to pray for him. They obeyed and prayed for his safety. Later the two discovered that at the precise moment they had been praying in New Zealand, Hayden had been spared by the firing squad in China.

Peter couldn't shake this story because it was hard for him to find a flaw in it. He knew the missionary and didn't believe the story had been fabricated in any way. For this reason, he was aware that there was a God and that this God was able to save people and was worthy of serving.

One night, travelling on a long road and coming down from a drug high, he found himself in the path of an oncoming car that had crossed the white line. There was no way the vehicle was going to miss him. He just had enough time to suck in his breath, before suddenly realizing that the car had gone on by and somehow, miraculously, it had missed him.

The next day he told his mother about what had happened.

"Oh?" she queried, "What time was that?" He told her and she said, "Well, Peter, I had been trying to go to sleep last night when I became overwhelmed with fear for your safety and realized that God was asking me to pray for you. I couldn't sleep until I got down on my knees and prayed."

Now the missionary's experience had become his own. He didn't want to know that God had intervened or was watching over him so he tried to erase it from his mind.

He was a fitter by trade and had gained his apprenticeship working in the railways but had slid further and further from a healthy lifestyle, as he pursued a dual career in drugs and alcohol.

Work in the railways at that time had been easy. It was no trouble spending half the day "out of it" on drugs, while faking the job. He once dropped a "trip" while working and was so stewed in his brain that he stood at his bench slowly moving his hands back and forth pretending to assemble whatever it was that was in front of him.

One day when he was working stoned he suddenly felt conscious of God and heard a voice imploring him, "Peter, why don't you become a Christian?"

"Oh no, not you, God! Go away."

Peter felt a solemn fear of an almighty God yet he won the battle and after he had wiped his brow from the effort, made a pact: "I'll become a Christian one day, when I am old, like, when I am 40."

From that day, things became messy for him. Pitching himself deeper into drugs and music, he immersed himself in the punk scene. Here life was about cynicism and hatred for society and normal suburban living. The hairstyles and clothing were uniforms of rebellion. One of the worst enemies was the hippie. This happy, flower-carrying individual was the antithesis of punk. Peter's ambition was to become a famous punk drummer.

Eventually Peter and his friends found themselves meddling with crime. The police as well as some of the underworld were looking for them. Life was starting to degenerate. Fear was replacing his teenage cockiness. Work had become difficult for him and after a series of jobs where he had no motivation to work or excel or achieve, he had found himself just capable of working as a store man in a paint shop where controls were lax. Some of the men stole paint. He had provided paint for a friend to paint his entire house. It was easy: load the work truck and drop it off. Write off the paint as spillage. Many did it.

At this time, Peter loved his girlfriend; she was an attractive young girl with a sharp mind who shared his love of music. She played the piano and her parents were Christian. Peter had it all worked out. One day they would become Christians, when they were much older, and they would play music for God together. One day.

One day came, but not the one Peter had planned. His

girlfriend started going out with his best friend. His emotions yo-yoed. His girlfriend confused him by crying and promising to come back, then rejecting him again and the repeating pattern was crippling him. On top of this was the fear of being caught by any of his recent enemies. His life was at rock bottom.

By now he was living in a flat on Grafton Road which was almost in the city itself, with five other drummers. He would walk across Grafton Bridge and contemplate what it might feel like to climb the barrier and throw himself down onto the motorway below.

During this time he tried to hold himself together and continued with his work. Then one day he was sitting in the "smoko" room during a break, with his head in his hands, feeling totally depressed and trying to think of how he could retrieve something of the situation. He was at a stalemate.

Again he heard a voice speaking to his mind, "Why don't you become a Christian?"

"Go away!" he wailed silently in his head. "I'm too weak to fight you off!"

He began to feel the unmistakable love of God descending on him. This time it was a revelation of love coming from Jesus and his sacrifice on the cross, that drew tears to his eyes. The feeling wouldn't leave and he returned to his work now struggling with his reaction. Before long he was rationalizing. "Why not become a Christian now? But I'm too young! Forty is so far off. Become a Christian? Why? What good would that do me? Why not give in to this love and become a Christian today?"

The debate wore on until Peter's argument turned more to "Why not? Why not become a Christian right now?" He thought that if he did decide to make this decision he might cry so he went off to the privacy of a toilet cubicle and sat down. Not knowing what to say he simply said, "OK, Lord. You win. I'm yours. Take me."

He sat for a few minutes and realized that he wasn't feeling anything. He wasn't crying; he just felt nothing. So that was it? He had made the decision and wasn't about to go back on it but it was almost an anticlimax.

He went back out into the washroom and as he came into the room he saw his reflection in the mirror. He was astonished! He had been used to seeing haunted eyes. His eyes had been empty, dark eyes like those he had often identified with on album covers of heavy, satanic bands. But now his eyes were full of light. He stood and saw coming from his own eyes the love that he had been sensing outside of him. He began to grin.

He couldn't stop grinning. A man came into the warehouse for some paint and Peter had an odd thought. "Instead of being sour and mean to this man I'm going to be nice!" This was a totally foreign idea and as the man came toward him, he felt himself smiling and as he smiled, the man smiled. It was almost awkward; he didn't know how to turn this thing off! He gave the man his paint and the man asked him if he would like some oranges. He was astounded. No one had given him anything on a job and now he was being given oranges!

He wasn't sure what he should do now that he was a Christian, but he was suspicious that a house full of punk drummer friends would not be sympathetic. Christians were worse than hippies. As his closest friend had snarled, "Christianity is the ultimate scapegoat!"

The first person he wanted to tell was his grandmother. He phoned her and told her. She didn't know whether to throw the phone in the air or fall on the floor. Suddenly he wanted to go and visit her and stay and talk and listen to her. So it was a day or two before he returned to his flat.

When he arrived home there was just one person there. They met in the hall and Peter could feel the infectious smile begin to play on his lips. As the smile grew, his friend's forehead wrinkled up in a puzzled expression as he too began to smile. Peter smiled and his friend smiled while Peter tried to think of how he was going to tell his friend. For some minutes they just stood in the hallway grinning until his friend broke the spell.

"Where've you been?"

"I ..."

"Yeah ..." his friend coaxed as Peter stumbled over his words to speak.

"I've become a Christian!"

Because they were already both smiling, his friend shook his head with the smile still on his face and said, "Good!"

It was a surprise. No one knocked his new direction. But he didn't know what he should do now, so he decided to do what none of them ever considered doing: he cleaned the flat and got up and made the others breakfast each day. In the meantime, someone had told him about the church in the Town Hall and since this was closest to where he was living, this was where he decided to look for other believers.

Now that he wanted more than anything to please God, it began to trouble him that he had stolen paint from his employer. He stopped this habit and instead began to save money to pay the employer back. Over these weeks he became an exemplary worker but now he was becoming unpopular because he wouldn't stop talking about Jesus. After he had saved the amount he thought he had stolen, he went to see his boss. He had $500, more than three weeks' wages at the time, to pay to him.

"I've come to tell you that I've become a Christian and that because of this I have to let you know that before this I'd been stealing paint, and now I want to pay you back."

The boss leaned back on his chair and sighed. He had already heard that this kid was becoming irritating with his proclamations of "Praise the Lord" and his persistent Bible bashing.

"Well, I need to think about this."

"Sure, but I want to pay you for the paint."

The boss took his money and then called him back later to tell him, "I'm going to have to sack you. Stealing is not acceptable and I'm going to have to make an example of you, so you're fired." The boss kept the $500 and Pete had been rewarded with the boot.

Peter refused to let this discourage him. He now knew that the Lord had plans for him and since he was in the Lord's hands, he need not worry. He would work at anything. He was reluctant to go back to his fitting trade, as his self-esteem was so low that he doubted he could hold a fitting job. This was how he found himself in the printing company, working for a cantankerous boss. He was employed as a general hand, operating a guillotine and sweeping the floor, making cardboard boxes, getting the lunches and making the tea. It was where God had placed him and he was going to learn new work habits and be the best cardboard box maker for God that he could be.

Chapter 17

Before long, I had heard Peter's story several times. The experiences he had been through went on playing with his broken emotions. He told me about his ex-girlfriend and how this broken relationship had driven him to the Lord. I secretly wondered how I would ever be able to tell anyone about my own journey of numerous broken relationships, several as painful as Pete had related, and all of them scarring.

I had to accept that Peter's way to Jesus had been remarkable. He thought that every Christian had begun with a direct revelation of Jesus and was quite surprised to discover people who had simply made a considered intellectual choice or who had made a decision after persuasion by a friend.

When he wasn't telling me his story, he was trying to educate me in the art of drumming. I was expert at appearing to listen. At least he wasn't grumbling or pouring out endless problems and phobias.

There was just one problem: it had become obvious that he was taking an interest in me. This didn't worry me too much, as I had no interest in him. Apart from the fact that he was a male, he also wasn't what I thought might be a match for me. For one thing, I was older by six and a half years. I was from a darker and more complex background. I had expected that if I ever had found a life partner it might be someone from a profession, a little older than me and hopefully, someone who was already reasonably well set up, someone more like Nicholas. If I was to ever marry, in obedience to the Lord, I expected it to look sensible.

I had lost a lot of time and a 22-year-old drummer who

boarded with friends and could carry everything he had in two or three bags didn't fit the bill. Not only that, his job was folding cardboard boxes and making tea. Everything about him was outside of my interest. He seemed to be reasonably bright at times, yet at times he seemed almost imbecilic. Sometimes he fumbled for words and when he conversed, it was as if his eyes were in a glazed, mindless stare. To top this off he was a fledgling Christian and I wanted someone I could admire for their spiritual maturity.

To put Peter off, I tried showing him the many grey hairs that were already sprouting on my head. This didn't seem to work. Still, he wasn't making a nuisance of himself and he wasn't sleazy or pushy, so I tolerated his visits and began to enjoy his friendship. After all, I found myself teaching him about his new faith and I enjoyed being useful. He would get over it.

The job ended in the printing company and Christmas was upon us. I had little money but a lot of time, so I made dough woven baskets and baked them and varnished them as gifts. To supplement my diet and live as much as I could on what I found, I had always eaten nasturtiums; the leaves and flowers went into salads and the seeds I could pickle. I dried and pickled hundreds of nasturtium seeds and sealed them in jars, as they were acceptable New Zealand substitutes for capers. These too were Christmas gifts.

I wanted to decorate my flat. For the last few years, Christmas hadn't been a festive event in my home. As long as I had been able to attend plenty of parties and Christmas booze events, I had been happy. Now I wanted my flat to look Christmassy but I had no money to buy decorations.

Having been a long-time hoarder I did have lots of strings of shiny beads, some crêpe paper and a few pieces of tinsel. I decided to design myself a tree using coat hangers. The first coat hanger could rest on a hook on the wall, then two hang side by side from this one, then three and lastly a row of four. I covered them with two different green lengths of crêpe paper and decorated my "tree" with beads and tinsel.

At night I lit a candle and felt very Christmassy as the beads sparkled on the tree. The little girl living next door thought it was the best Christmas tree she had ever seen. Most adults observed my tree with speechless amusement or a horrified perplexity. Peter fell into the latter but was too polite to mention it at the time.

Molly came to visit one night and I lit my candle in honour of her visit. As I had always been a talker, it was difficult for this girl to get a word in edgeways. In the end she shouted at me just in time for me to turn and see the candle had burned to the end and the plastic holder, painted with silver, was on fire, with the plastic melting fast.

"You're so weird," Molly moaned.

The silver became a fine dust that settled everywhere and took me weeks to finally clean away.

I continued to renew my friendship with Loran. She had known me in Christchurch and had been a friend of mine and Sharon's. It was good to have someone I could talk with who had been an old friend. Loran was now married but she met with me to encourage my faith. She was one of those incredibly practical people who seemed able to foresee a person's needs.

I had managed a basic diet of the cheapest food for my cats but this was fast running out toward Christmas Day and my new work was still a few days away. Then Loran sent me a parcel for Christmas. It was a huge box of cat food including some raw meat! I couldn't believe I had been so blessed by God through her. I hadn't told her I was low on cat food and now they too could have something special for Christmas! I had always known God loved animals and especially mine, as he knew how much I loved them too.

On Christmas Day, my dear, little, aged neighbour, Martha, with her teeth poked out, came for lunch along with my parents, and Hydra, who was still trying to follow Jesus at this stage. It was a humble party. We sat around my coffee table and it felt like a real Christmas to me.

Peter was away visiting his mother far away in the north. She lived at Cooper's Beach, in a lovely coastal town. I noticed wistfully that I was missing his smiling face and his wholesome outlook. It was through this time that Hydra and Helen had visited with the stolen bread, hoping to choke this new "saint". It was also through this holiday time that I had been told I was not able to have a Bible study with my friends and I had to watch them swept back into their old lives.

Little did I know that as Peter walked and prayed on his beach walks, he was asking the Lord if we were meant to be together. He became confident that the Lord was going to give him "the desires of his heart".[15]

Work began in the travel office and at least I now had a longer temporary job. I could now earn enough to buy food for my furry companions.

As the ten days came to an end I was aware that Peter would be back on a Tuesday and I said to Loran, "You know, this kid Peter is so predictable. When he gets back, he'll wait for a few hours and then ring me as if he has just casually decided to catch up."

The phone rang at exactly the time I predicted.

"Hello, Peter." I couldn't help but smile. But I was glad he was back.

It felt comfortable chatting to my friend. I didn't feel quite so alone now he was in Auckland. I just had to make sure he didn't cross any boundaries.

The next day I was helping a new Christian acquaintance to shift house. This girl knew Peter as well so he sauntered along the road to join us. He was just wearing shorts, as it was a searingly hot day in mid-summer. I watched him coming along the road, munching on an ice cream, and thought, "Hmm, he's managed to get a great tan over summer. He's got quite a nice bod' for a little guy. Skinny legs, but he's pretty muscly under those stripy T-shirts he wears!"

I was at once on guard. Thoughts like this were exactly how I had fallen into trouble on more than one occasion and I was determined never to go that way again. What was more confusing was that Peter was male. I hadn't had a thought like this toward a male in years.

Peter, in the meantime, was obvious in his pursuit but it was amusing to watch. He finished work about an hour before I did but I would board my bus and every night he would jump onto the same one, getting on at the bus stop at the bottom of town.

"Hi!" he would exclaim in surprise. "I've been shopping for a CD I wanted." He would dangle the CD in its bag at me. Or there would be some story of being caught up talking or some other distraction that meant each night that he had just "happened" to get onto my bus.

One night we were travelling home and he said, "Do you ever go down to the little bays around the harbour after work?"

"Yep, sometimes. I go down to pray or to read."

"Me too."

I thought about the night I had sat reading from Song of Songs and how a man who could have been the model for the poem had come down to the empty beach and had stripped totally naked as I watched from my perch on the hillside.

Peter broke into my thoughts. "Do you know the bay where there is an old pier out over the sea?"

"Yep, I know the one."

"Well, I'm going for a walk there tonight."

"Oh yeah." I made myself a mental note to keep well away from the pier tonight.

About 8pm, Peter came wandering up my road. I was outside petting one of my cats. He stopped at the end of my path and looked up at me with a grumpy face.

"Hi, Peter," I called. "You want a coffee?"

I couldn't give him any hope; he just wasn't in my future plan. We were back to a comfortable friendship in a short time and he was happily telling me about some drumming technique again, so I figured he had thawed out.

Chapter 18

As summer wore on, Peter found his way to my flat almost every evening, or we went to something church-related and our friendship grew. He was harmless and I could see qualities in him that I hadn't at first noticed. He had the same focussed passion that I did for following Jesus and that counted more than anything.

One evening over coffee, I told Peter all about my earlier love for Greg and explained that it was impossible for me to ever love another man. I thought that this would be enough to put him off, but he just smiled and continued the pursuit.

Before I had noticed it, Peter had grown on me to become like a comfortable cat in my life. It started to bother me that I enjoyed his company more and more and I didn't want this to become something silly. Now we met after work each day and had coffee before travelling home together. Sometimes we did walk to the bays or visited each other's homes.

One night we had decided to go to an evening for young adults organized by the church. As a real treat, Peter's flat-mate would sometimes lend him his old van. It was a rickety, grey monster nicknamed "the Rat", but it was wheels. To get to the venue we would have to drive. For some reason, at the last minute, we couldn't borrow the Rat. I had arrived at Peter's with my friend Dinah so instead, we decided to go for a walk in the local park and take the flatmate's two German shepherd dogs.

It was a fine, warm summer's evening and the park was pleasant. I noticed that Peter loved these animals and had an authority with them. I thought he looked kind of cute in his denim jacket as he masterfully dog-handled them. We returned to his flat and had coffee. Somehow we ended up having a play fight and laughing and tussling in the lounge. Dinah laughed at our antics and I tried to display some of my "big time wrestling" moves that never had worked for me in the past. Peter was much stronger than I had thought.

Returning home, I was horrified. That was far too much body contact for comfort. This was not going well. It was time I stepped back and set some boundaries. What was Peter thinking? I wasn't going to play this game.

I phoned my sister and she annoyed me by passing on a verse of scripture that she felt was for me. "Those who are joined in the Spirit are one."[16] I was infuriated; this scripture wasn't helpful.

The next Tuesday night I went to church deliberately, avoiding Peter. Strangely, he hadn't contacted me. I sat downstairs as we always sat in the balcony. I sat with Lottie. I looked up as the meeting began and Peter was in the balcony. He saw me and waved a friendly greeting. I smiled with a distant and hopefully cool smile and concentrated on the meeting. At the end of the evening, I suddenly remembered that we always walked home together, as there was no bus that went my way this late. I looked around, but Peter had gone!

I was mortified. Peter was avoiding me! But I was avoiding him! How dare he? I was so flustered, I took a taxi and found myself crying on the way home, with annoyance and rejection. Crying over Peter Baskett! It was ridiculous.

Thursday night I went to our home group and kept my distance from Peter, but it was obvious that he was distancing himself from me too. Instead of having Peter walk me home, I asked Lottie to drop me off. On the way home she asked, "Why aren't you walking home with Peter?"

"Well, Lottie, I'm trying to keep away from Peter right now."

"Why?" she demanded in shades of her earlier persona.

"Well, it just isn't a good thing."

"Why not? I thought you two were getting on well."

"I don't want this to become a relationship. It just wouldn't be right. If I was going to get that close to a guy, it would have to be for marriage. I just don't want to make any mistakes any more."

"So what's wrong with Peter?"

"Lottie! Peter is six and a half years younger than me."

"So?" I had expected her to be sensible and agree with me.

I managed to hold off until Friday when I could no longer cope with the tension. It was hurting my pride to think that this skinny kid was sanctimoniously keeping his distance from me, when I was the one who was meant to be evading him! I phoned him from my work.

"Hello, stranger!" he replied cheerily.

"What do you mean, 'stranger'?" I blurted. "You've been avoiding me!"

"Yes, I guess I have."

"Well, I'm avoiding you too!" Once out, it all seemed so adolescent.

"Do you want to do coffee after work?"

"Sure I do!" I pouted.

We went to one of our favourite coffee shops and it was as if nothing had happened. We talked about why we had both backed off and I felt safer again. It shocked me that I also felt happy that we were friends again and that Peter had meant so much to me.

Over the next week, my emotions became tangled. This young guy was getting under my skin. I liked his laugh, he was easy to be with and more than anything, we enjoyed our new life in Jesus; each new revelation was like discovering gems. Jesus was the basis of our conversation and connection.

The next Saturday dawned sunny and cloudless. The suburbs where we lived had many quaint houses and on a walk along some of the narrow streets we would admire cottages draped in wisteria and gardens with rose bushes and jasmine. This day was perfect for a stroll along the lanes. We wandered from Peter's home along the romantic streets. I had a compulsive urge to take his hand. He was my friend and I was enjoying the day. I reached for his hand and grabbed it, then tried to ignore the feeling of utter stupidity that came with my action. But it was done: we were walking along holding hands. It felt wrong. It felt absurd.

After about five minutes we stopped and Peter said with a quizzical smile, "What are you doing?"

"I don't know." I shrugged. "I just wanted to hold your hand."

"Me too."

"But I feel stupid."

"OK, so let's stop doing that."

This was so uncomfortable. I felt relief. I had no intention of starting anything with this young guy. We walked on for some minutes. It still felt wrong.

"I still want to hold your hand," I said.

"OK."

We clutched hands and walked on. We came to the end of the lanes and found ourselves on the corner of a main road. I was suddenly terrified that people would see us. Maybe one of my old friends might see me, holding hands with a guy.

We walked on down to a small park. Heading down the path, the sun shone with what seemed like an unusual golden light. The path wound down the middle of soft, green grass dotted with daisies. It was becoming comic. An old lady passed us and smiled benevolently, then absurdly, a butterfly fluttered across a sunbeam in front of our path and we laughed.

"OK!" I shouted to the sky. "Enough!"

We walked to the water's edge, under the Harbour Bridge. I felt happy. Maybe this was meant to be?

We fell into talking about our future hopes and dreams. Mine were to leave these shores as soon as I could and adventure into the world. Peter loved Auckland and could think of nowhere better in the world to be. I checked my fast-moving thoughts. I loved summer, beaches, light clothes and barbecues. Peter loved winter, scarves, hats and football. A shadow drew across the idyllic day.

Sunday we walked home from church hand in hand. Now it was a little more comfortable. We sat out on the old wooden porch in the sun on a big comfortable sofa. We had managed to sit tangled together and I realized that Pete was going to kiss me. He was slower than I would have been but this time, I wasn't going to be the initiator. Finally his lips touched mine and instead of chemistry, a blanket of peace enveloped us both. It was as if we had entered a celestial cloud full of angels. I knew the difference between adrenalin and God's tangible presence and we were in his presence.

This sense stayed with us for three days. Maybe, I considered, we will live in this wonderful bubble of God's happiness forever? Marriage to Pete looked an option. I had no intention of stepping into a silly and transient relationship at this stage.

On the third day, we went to our favourite coffee shop and Pete sat opposite me telling me his testimony, perhaps for the sixteenth time. This time I was listening with rapt attention, holding his hands across the table and feeling a wonderful flow of God's love between us. As Peter came to the part where his girlfriend ran off with his best friend, he began to weep. Soon his head was on the table and he was crying like a baby. I could still feel the love of Christ flowing from my hands into Peter but my mind had shut off my own emotions. "What's with this guy?" I now worried to myself. "He's so weak! Look at him there, a mess! Maybe he isn't really in his right mind!

What do I really know about this kid?" I didn't know that males could feel deep hurt.

As God's love flowed from me to Pete, he was receiving an emotional healing but I didn't know that. I just saw this blubbering young man in front of me and all the illusions of happiness, the rays of sunshine, butterflies and angel kisses had dissolved in a damp, gloomy cloud.

After coffee Pete wanted to go up to a park on a hill above the city streets, to pray about our future. We strolled up the hill and Pete was now elated. As miserable as he had been a few minutes before, he was now bubbling and talkative and happy. We came to a park bench and sat. Peter prayed, "Farver, please knit us together and make us one."

In my mind, I prayed, "Lord, please put a rain cheque on this one!"

Lying in bed that night I started to argue with God. How had this mess happened? What had I been thinking? This guy couldn't even speak decent English! I had to get out of this fast! But he was my best friend. In a short time, we had become close companions. He was the only one around me that I felt I could relate to who didn't drain me with his problems. I didn't want to lose his friendship but this could not work!

I lost sleep, tossing and turning and arguing with heaven. By day, I would meet with Pete and continue to walk hand in hand, while beating him with my words.

"I can't marry you, Pete."

"I'm not forcing you to marry me."

That was true; who had spoken of marriage? "But, you see, I have career hopes and if I marry you, chances are that I will have to lay these aside, especially if we have a family. And then I'd have to get behind what you do – you fold cardboard boxes!"

"Sure, and if the Lord wants me to fold cardboard boxes for the rest of my life, then that's what I am going to do!"

"Yeah, but that's no comfort to me," I added, "and you are not as intelligent as me." I had always measured intelligence by communication and had mostly favoured people from arts or commerce backgrounds. I had never had much time for left-brained individuals and knew little about people like Pete.

He didn't fight me; he just continued to love me. This made me more uncomfortable because although I didn't want to let him go, he just wasn't seeing my problem. In the end, I was blatantly telling him that, frankly, he was "dumb". I couldn't marry someone who was "dumb". A mutual friend asked me one night during this time if Peter was "backward". This fed my insecurity because when he talked to me, his eyes were slightly vacant and the stumbling speech was evident.

I phoned my sister again. Once again she had a verse of scripture to give me, "Let a righteous man rebuke me, let a good man reprove me, it shall not break my head."[17] This was not helpful! It was saying to me that no matter how much I beat up on Pete, he would not break and that he was my "head"! Certainly he was losing the image of "weakness" as he took words blow by blow from my blunt and insulting tongue.

I said to him one day during this time, "The trouble with you, Pete, is that you think that marriage will be a bed of roses!"

He replied, "What makes you fink I would imagine after these last few weeks that marriage to you could be a bed of roses?" He had a point.

Finally one night as I wrestled with God, I said, "OK, Lord, I have tried everything else. If you want me to marry this guy I will accept him, 'cardboard boxes' and all!"

The next day, Pete was shaving when all of a sudden a thought dropped into his head. "I want you to go to a technical institute and do a diploma in engineering." Pete was delighted and astonished and couldn't wait to tell me that evening after work. He raced into my office.

"Guess what? The Lord spoke to me this morning!"

"Yeah ... " I said warily. So many times, Peter's revelations had been "He told me how much he loves me!" or "He is showing me how lucky I am to have time to praise him while I am working!" This time he told me about the prompt for further study. He had my attention. The Lord had my attention and I had some hope that there might be more of a brain in there after all.

Coinciding with my attacks, Pete was being more and more victimized in his workplace. His boss shouted at him frequently and the attacks were more malicious. Goliath had dragged an army of other workers into his pool of revilers. Now voices shouted at Pete all day that he couldn't sweep floors properly or make a decent cup of tea. He just took each insult and thanked the Lord that he was able to absorb their hate, while retaining his peace. He went out of his way for these men and volunteered to get the lunches and perform any menial task of service. Nothing he could do was right. The accusation became a chorus, "You're dumb!"

One Tuesday night at this time, we had been to a concert and had returned to my flat for coffee. Pete told me about the increasing siege against him at work so I agreed to pray for him. I went and stood by him and put my hand on his head and began to pray.

Pete told me that as I began to pray he remembered something. He remembered that as a child in his country school, he had felt inferior. It was a tiny school, made up by just four families. He became angry that he was fatherless and that the one other child in his class of two always bettered him. So he became bitter and decided that he was "dumb". His mother took him to a child psychiatrist as she and his grandmother had noticed his speech deteriorating. The psychiatrist said that he had an above average IQ and that there was no reason for this change in him. Now as we prayed, he let go of the bitterness.

He felt as if he had been wearing a stocking on his head, like a cat-burglar. As we prayed he felt as if the stocking was being taken off his head.

After we had prayed he told me that because of his inferiority, he had felt unable to look people in the eye. So he had devised a way to be able to look at a person but make his focus just a few inches from their face. This gave him the now familiar vacant stare. He had been doomed all these years to appear "dumb".

From the next day onward at work, Pete's workmates mysteriously never once uttered the accusing words again. His speech began to normalize and he was able to look people in the eye.

One winter's night soon after, I had been about to return home from visiting Pete. By this time he had moved in with an older Anglican lady and he lived on the landing in her two-storied house. Our talk had been about Peter's drug experiences and I was getting tired. When he first smoked marijuana, he said he had blacked out and when he woke up he had noticed that his eyes had looked tormented.

I was getting tired so I said I was going home. But Pete was now feeling agitated and said he felt sick. He asked me to pray for him. I suggested that he probably needed to go to see Bill Subritzky, a well-known ministry, since Peter looked like he needed to be free from something spiritual. He was persistent so I agreed to pray for peace for him.

Peter sat on a dining room chair and I dutifully closed my eyes and began to quietly pray. Within seconds I heard a snarling and growling coming from Peter! I opened my eyes and with shock saw that he had crumpled into a tight, buckled position; his hands were clamped in an unmistakable demonic way, his fingers forced outward rigidly. Fear gripped me for a few seconds. "Sons of Sceva!"[18] I thought, remembering the Bible story of the men who had been torn by demons, through ignorantly wading in to cast them out without the authority of Christ.

"I can't do this! I'm a woman!"

Then a burning rage rose up inside me. I knew what it was to go through this type of experience and I could see that the devil had my man in pain! How dare he! I then realized that this ministry had nothing to do with me. I couldn't cast out an ant! This was the work of the Holy Spirit and I was simply the person on the spot. The least could put a thousand to flight if the power of the Lord was with them![19] So I began to pray with the righteous anger I felt coming from within.

The Anglican lady was at that moment sitting in her bath upstairs when she heard the ruckus. She immediately got out and started to phone all her Christian friends. "Quick! Pray! It sounds like they've stirred up something demonic downstairs in my dining room. Pray!"

Peter writhed across the floor and hissed but after some time, he was quiet and totally free. We knew that whatever had hooked onto him when he was doing drugs had now gone.

Chapter 19

I was still not so sure that Pete was going to be able to partner me. I was well aware that I was strong-willed and sometimes caustic. He was such a "kid". It didn't seem quite right. I was discipling him from what I had learned at Bible College and he was asking all the questions. The Bible said that if he was my husband, I should go home and ask him the questions![20] I agreed with the notion of marrying a man who might be at least my equal.

One afternoon we had been praying and enjoying our relationship that was now building on Jesus. It was the oddest relationship I had ever been in. It was warm, affectionate but not sexually driven. I liked Pete as a person, so I overlooked the fact that he was a guy. I couldn't say I was feeling great passion for him, but our mutual passion for the Lord was drawing us closer and closer as a couple. It was so outside of anything I had experienced before, that I had to throw out my preconceived beliefs about romance, love and human relationships.

Suddenly I remembered that I had promised to go and visit Thad and listen to his complaints. Arriving at his place we squeezed onto one of his old couches. He had managed to fit more and more into his tiny bedsit from foraging at inorganic rubbish collections. There were at least three layers of carpet beneath our feet. Thad was drinking and soon Hydra arrived with another friend and they joined the party. A neighbour, a young man, was sitting in a chair next to us. We started to talk to him and tell him about Jesus. The more we talked, the more we could feel that wonderful sense of the presence of God. We talked for several hours and then decided that it was time to go. The drinkers had been getting rowdier and less stable, falling around the room and we had said all we could say.

Pete walked me home. We started down the street talking excitedly about how Jesus had been there, and praying for the young man we had been talking to. We could still feel a strong sense of God.

Something seemed a bit odd. I stopped and looked at Pete. He had grown physically about six inches and was now a lot taller than me! We stood apart and he looked down at his legs and remembered one of his tall, thin friends and mused on how this must be how he felt. We measured the difference in height that was now obvious to us both, and yet neither of us thought it was frightening or uncanny. It just felt almost normal.

We went on walking and before we came to my flat, I noticed that Pete had gone back to his usual, short height. He was naturally only a few inches taller than I was. It wasn't until we sat with coffee in my flat, that we realized that something out of the ordinary had happened and we both felt shocked. We had no witnesses, but to this day, both of us can remember this event clearly. To me it spoke faith into my fears. The Lord was saying that nothing is impossible with him[21] and that Pete would grow past me.

I worried too that God seemed to want me to be in ministry. How could I explain this to Pete without appearing stupid as this looked so unlikely. So I said to the Lord, "Well, if Pete really is my new 'plan A' partner, then you'll have to tell him!"

The next day, Pete was praying about me while making some deliveries in his work van. As he prayed, a scripture came to his mind, "A prophet is not accepted in his own land or amongst his own people."[22] After shunting this obscure scripture away it came back again more forcefully. Suddenly he was awake. He rushed into my office in his lunch break.

"I know about you!" he yelled across the office, and I was glad I was alone. "The Lord has told me! You are going to speak for him! You have been called!" He was almost jumping for joy. I now had to explain that these things were serious. Pete was about to start on a new learning curve.

Now we had so much evidence that we were going in the right direction that I could see no reason why we just couldn't get on with the process and get married. We had talked of this but Pete hadn't yet proposed! I had emphatically stated that if we had a wedding, I would not be a bride. There would have to be another way to be at the church and do the ceremony without me having to stand with all those eyes looking at me. Then I remembered that Pete was an only child and that if he didn't have a real wedding, then his mother would never have that pleasure, so somehow I would have to endure it.

On a walk home in mid-autumn, we stopped in a park. I sat on the park bench and Pete asked me if I would marry him. It was a still night but when I said "Yes", a strong wind came from nowhere and blew the tree we were sitting under and rushed past our faces. This was just how we felt too. It was terrifying. What had we done? It was the most serious, scary agreement I had ever made. I was fully aware that I was giving my life in companionship to this young fellow to the end of our living days.

The old ladies in the home group, led by Lottie, said, "About time! The way he looked at you!"

Not long after this, Peter annoyed me by looking into my kitchen cupboards and noting that I had a collection of second-hand plates, a set of old cutlery, some glasses and a few essential homewares.

"Hey! We're pretty well set up!" he announced. What was this "we" part? All he was going to add was a cast iron frying pan and his drum kit!

The next time we were in church I felt the Lord mentally

nudge me as I was singing an old hymn, "All to Jesus, I surrender." I was singing with such sentimental ardour. "If you mean what you are singing," the impression came into my mind, "then what about my servant Peter here? I want you to give it all to him!"

I was appalled. Well, he could have everything except my guitar. Later I could have slammed my guitar over his head, as he spent hours playing one or two chords percussively, as rhythm was far more interesting to him than melody! At least my possessions included my cats and he would have to learn not to stand on their tails if they were to become part of his domain.

Peter always says that I got the better deal since his frying pan was a promise of his great cooking to come! I had a picture of marriage being something of a grind, where I would have to be the little domestic servant, cooking and cleaning. Little did I know that Pete would provide me with gourmet meals for years to come!

We were too poor to buy an engagement ring and I didn't care for diamonds and jewels anyway. This changed a little as my workmates began to taunt me. "Isn't that boyfriend of yours rich enough to buy you a ring?" they snorted. I didn't answer them or try to straighten them out but it chafed and I wanted to at least wear something as evidence of the betrothal. I had once had a small ring with two hearts that my mother had given me. I loved this little ring but I had lost it and even Dinah's unusual talent had failed me. I remained without a ring.

As a formality we went to see our area pastor. This young pastor had known me for years. He had come to know Jesus through my sister and had been close friends with Brent, the boyfriend whose heart I had crushed when I left to go to Bible College. He knew all about my past and no doubt feared for this nice young man I had in tow. He said that he wasn't happy with the two-month engagement we had planned. He wanted us to wait.

I was furious. I had dreamed just the night before, a vivid dream where I woke and saw my lounge light on. I had run out to see who was there. In this dream, this pastor was in my lounge looking under a chair. I shouted indignantly, "What are you doing?"

"You just can't come back and be so good as you appear. You must be hiding something!"

Sitting in his office I knew that he preached about the power of Jesus to change people but found it difficult to believe that even God could change a lesbian. And I was angry because he was plain wrong!

Outside, Pete said, "I think it's right to just wait. The Lord will give us a date."

"Sure," I said evenly, not wanting to appear rebellious. Inside I was seething. I felt humiliated as Pete laughed at me and said, "You fell off your pedestal there, didn't you!" I was annoyed that he had put me on the pedestal in the first place and was in no mood to be congenial.

My peace evaporated and I tossed and turned, sleepless at night. It wasn't my fault, I argued. I was being compliant, wasn't I? It was just that I needed to organize this event and a girl needed a date to work toward. Besides, I lived alone in a small flat and Pete was boarding. It seemed a nonsense to me that we shouldn't just merge our lives right now and get on with life.

I did everything within my power to try to regain my peace with God. I went into the countryside and spent a weekend with Rachael at her parents' new home, but I didn't sleep. I came back early on the Sunday afternoon and met Pete by a bus stop. We had planned to go and visit his grandmother for Sunday lunch. Peter had just been to church.

"We had a good message this morning."

"Mmmm?"

"Yes, and I think it was for you! The pastor talked about how you can be submissive on the outside but inwardly rebelling and I think that this is what you're doing!"

He had exposed me and taken me by surprise. I had no other choice but to let go of my "rights". Peter didn't quite have the courage to tell me that the other impression he had felt was that God was going to somehow bless us with an engagement ring if I dealt with my attitude.

Gran fed us an old-fashioned roast dinner then sent us into her living room. Pete came into the room with his hand behind his back.

"Guess what? Gran has given us this!" He revealed a ring box and inside was a lovely, antique ring with three stones. Then Pete told me what he had thought in the morning and Gran came in to explain her part. She was always neatly dressed and wore her grey hair in a rolled bun captured in a small scarf and today she was wiping her hands on her floral apron.

"While I was praying this morning," said this little lady with her slight Scottish accent, "the Lord told me to give you this ring. Peter's father made it, you know."

It wasn't until after we were married that I heard the full story. I had not been too surprised that Peter's father had made this ring since he had been a manufacturing jeweller. I supposed that Gran had many such rings.

When Gran was a young woman with her two little children and her husband out of work, she had struggled to feed her family. It was the Depression and the family had been forced to live in a tiny, makeshift house, in a temporary housing area around a swamp. One day, to feed the family, Gran had pawned her engagement ring. Her son, Pete's father, had not forgotten this act of sacrifice and when he was working he had saved and bought small amounts of gold and platinum to fashion a replacement ring for his mother.

Finally, he had enough to make the ring and the bridge. He worked for hours making intricate patterns to hold the stones, but he was impatient. It would take him a long time to put in diamonds the size he needed to finish the ring. He couldn't wait to give his mother the ring, so he put in spinnels, semi-precious gems, and brought it home. Within weeks, he would be dead in Gran's arms, losing his life to a heart attack at the age of 40. The ring was Gran's dearest possession.

This was the ring that Gran had now given me. Her face beamed as she told me the story, "... and you know, Shirley? When the Lord told me to give you this ring and I did, those spinnels turned into diamonds for me!"

Chapter 20

Eventually we did feel happy about a date and we worked toward the 24th September, 1983. Later Geoff and Karen, our home group leaders, gave us a verse of scripture from the book of Haggai that was full of promise. We wrote it on our wedding programme: "From this day forward, I will bless you, says the Lord."[23] Many things now fell into place for us. We had little money but the Lord made up for it by providing everything.

A week before the wedding we went to visit a pastor I had known in my earlier Christian days. He offered to pray for me since I had such a phobia about being a bride. After he had prayed a few appropriate words, he then began to encourage us with words that he hadn't expected to say. He said that I was called to ministry and that Pete would be my support. I was a little amazed as I knew this man to not particularly agree with women in ministry! Then he used the same words that Peter Morrow had used so many years before, that I would walk before kings, and nations would come to me. The promise remained and later as I took teams to other countries and ministered in many different cultures, these words would come to pass.

Just before the wedding, I was to meet Peter's mother. I had met her and Peter's grandmother briefly months before. I had thought that they were a rather dour pair. I had imagined they were looking me up and down, disapproving of me. I had thought at the time, "Don't look at me like that. I'm not interested in your boy!"

Three days before the wedding Peter's mother had arrived from the north. Peter had organized for us to have dinner together at a favourite Chinese restaurant. I was nervous. Just before we got to the restaurant, Pete said, "Oh, by the way, I've told my mother all about you."

"Good … of course, you don't mean, ALL about me?"

"Sure!"

"About the way I was!" I spluttered. "You've got to be joking! There's no way she could accept that! Don't you get it? You're her only son; it's bad enough that you're being married off to an older woman! There's no way she could accept this! No mother could!" If I was nervous before, now I was terrified.

"You don't know my mother."

The meal was barely over when Peter excused himself. I was frozen with terror. How could he do this to me? No sooner had he gone from the table but his mother leaned over and said with an expressionless face, "Now that Peter has gone, there is something I want to say to you!"

My heart sank.

"I just want to be first to welcome you into our family! You have no idea how much I'm looking forward to getting to know you. I'm so pleased with Peter's choice!"

I had nothing to say but began to breathe again. This was the start of a relationship that feels similar to that of the Bible pair, Ruth and Naomi.[24] I didn't know mothers could be like this.

If I hadn't renewed my friendship with Loran, now to be my bridesmaid, everything could have been a mess. This friend should have been in business as a wedding organizer. She was meticulous and generous, down to sending me muesli in jars to ensure I would keep healthy and buying my shoes and looking after other details for the wedding. She would have to buy her own dress as bridesmaid and so colour and style was her choice. What did I know about weddings? I had made it a lifetime goal to have as little to do with weddings as I could, and these events rarely occurred in my old scene.

I found material at half price and Molly came into her own, as she was a fashion designer and seamstress. She made my dress as my gift. We didn't know that it was common to use a quaint church and still have your own minister so we booked the plain, old chapel at the top of Queen Street that the church used, partly as an office and for smaller meetings.

Loran organized flowers and every small detail. At the time, Loran was attending St Paul's Anglican Church. It is a lovely old historic stone church and the vicar had just finished freshly painting the crypt with its gothic arches and had varnished the honey-coloured wooden floor. Once again, because of Loran, we were able to book this for our reception. She organized trestle tables and we covered these with sheets and decorated them with jars of flowers from Loran's garden.

Friends volunteered to take snapshots and we were grateful, as we couldn't afford film. Loran's husband was a car salesman, and he "borrowed" a white Mercedes to use as our wedding car for the morning! One of my gay male hairdressing friends wanted to do my hair. On the day of the wedding, his leg was freshly cased in plaster after a car accident and he had to stand with his leg perched on a chair, while he turned my fuzzy mop into curls, entwined with tiny gypsophila flowers.

The wedding was humble, but the presence of Jesus was rich. One of Peter's cousins, a biker, said that it was at our wedding that he first sensed the love of God. He later came to know Jesus.

On the day, I was amazed to find that I felt nothing but peace and actually enjoyed all the eyes on me! Small tears were glistening in Peter's eyes as I came to him at the altar. Later, he infuriated me when I asked him what he was feeling as he saw me approach and he replied, "Sorry, I was too busy holding back my tears as I had just had a revelation of the love of the Lord!" Upstaged by Jesus! What could I say?

I can't say I was looking forward to the wedding night. It

was still not the most exciting thing to realize that I had now promised myself, body and emotions, to a male. I was going to try to make this thing work. I had chosen first to obey the leading of the Lord. And now it was a choice to reorient myself to heterosexual love. I figured that if women in arranged marriages might only meet their husbands on the night of the wedding and could learn to love, then I could too.

One of the first things Pete had to do was prune those wires in the horrible old mattress, which would have to suffice until we could afford a new bed!

I had been married to Pete for at least two years before I really noticed that he was good-looking. By then I had talked him into growing his hair. From the shaved, punk style he had worn to a long, almost hippie length, it was a transformation of outlook that was almost more radical than I had undergone. I now saw his brilliant, blue eyes and his strong chiselled jaw line and as he grew into his mid-twenties, he filled out to have a well-built and masculine figure. I often wondered how I had caught such an attractive man!

By marrying Pete, in obedience to what I felt God had said, I had been forced to re-evaluate all my ideas of "chemistry", love and fulfilment in relationships. I hadn't married Pete to "be" fulfilled, but to partner him in our mutual walk with God. There was almost no chemistry, yet that would surface eventually. At first it was mostly a great deal of respect and fondness.

The respect came because I was praying one day about marriage and what the Lord expected of me. I didn't want to give up all my rights as an individual and become some sort of dishcloth. The Lord drew my attention to a verse of scripture that formed the base of my interaction with Pete. To choose to respect him was the key to loving him.[25]

Pete prayed about his part as a Christian husband. His punk roots had not given him any better understanding about love any more than my old life had done. Once he bought me a flower under the duress of the mocking girls in my office and, rather than being embarrassed handing it to me, he left it on the seat where he had been waiting, saying to me as he got up, "You've left something!"

He now wanted to obey the scripture that would become his base for love, to love me "as Christ loved the church".[26] He figured that since Jesus showed his love by service, even to the point of washing his disciples' feet, then his role was to lay down his life for me.

Being married to Pete didn't mean that I had one day decided, "Well, now I am heterosexual." I hadn't even considered debating whether I could be heterosexual; I just happened to meet this human that the Lord made very obvious was to be my partner for life. He was male, so I had better get used to it! In my Bible readings I had soon realized that love was more about yielding our own rights and dying to selfishness, whether this was in marriage or friendship or family. Forgiveness and humility were the building blocks.

Earlier, I had built a lot of my survival techniques around popular success formulas. As baby-boomers, we had been taught solidly that the most important person is Number One – myself. The Bible now taught me that there was only one Number One, Jesus Christ. The world had said I should build self-esteem and work toward self-realization. The Bible now told me to die to self! The Lord had a number of ways of ensuring that I would have plenty of opportunities to practise dying to self!

One time, before we married, I had been on the bus home with Pete, when he clashed with my sensibilities over something. I had my dignity! Why should I bend to anyone? I had made my feelings clear before Pete got off the bus. I was indignant as I huffed and puffed in my defence to the Lord back home in my flat. Then the Lord spoke to me with an uninvited rebuke, "What do you know of dignity? You have no dignity! But if you let me, I can teach you what dignity is. The first thing you must do is phone Peter and apologize for your bad behaviour!"

The voice of God is gentle but never compromising. We can ignore these invasive prompts but I was so aware that I had a long way to go, to get from where I had been living in disobedience, ignorance and pride, to where the Lord wanted me to be. My expectations had to die along with my pride.

Having received such a wonderful scripture for our wedding day, we expected everything to change and our lives to be rosy from the 24th of September. Yet, the Lord's view of blessing is far more eternal. Temporal blessing is good, but far inferior to his intention for us. From the 24th of September, even until today, over 20 years later, our lives have been full of testing and trial. Through the "blessing" and wealth of our suffering in so many ways, we have become rich in knowing Jesus. Our marriage has been strengthened and matured and our love has grown into a firm union that has survived so much.

For months after our wedding an old friend would bump into someone in the gay world and would say, "Have you heard the news about Shirley?"

"Yeah! She went religious!"

"No! She's married!"

Chapter 21

Only a few more events need to be told to complete the story of this journey out of lesbianism. After a few years, I was managing a corporate travel agency for a bank. It was the best job I had ever had and life was more secure. We had bought our first home with more help from God. Pete had finished his studies and was now qualified as a technical engineer.

My obsession with women had long died. Now I had a greater obsession to replace any longing I had ever had. Within a year of marriage we had been told that we would never have children. This news had been more painful than anything I had yet experienced. I had so desired a baby and now my arms would be empty and every friend who joyously told me of their first baby would send me into days of depression.

Not only was my hope destroyed, but I also had to stick to my marriage vow and learn to love Peter just for himself. He was all I had. Deep down, I was still dreaming that another human could fulfill me, only this time my hope had been in the right to motherhood and a baby I could bond to. I tried bribing the Lord. I then attempted to deal with anything that would lead me to "obsessively" love a child. I mined for every sin, every attitude that I thought might be holding back the blessing that I saw come so easily to others. I prayed and begged for a miracle like Hannah.[27]

In my pain, I lost friends who saw my reactions as selfish or judged me for the way I was handling this tragedy. Some were my closest friends. I was now reliving the trial that my own mother had had with my brother Ronnie but in different circumstances. Ironically, we were living two doors away from my early childhood home, at the time we learned of our infertility.

Nothing in medical science could help us and at the time, the waiting list was so long for couples desiring adoption that when I contacted the department, I was told to "go away. You are too old". I was 35 by the time Pete felt ready to consider adoption and by then it was too late. It wasn't until I was in my forties that the unwritten policy was relaxed and we could go on the list. But after many years of hope and hope dashed and being on this list, a baby was never to be our joy. This pain simply opened my eyes to see things in a more eternal perspective.

In my lowest moments, heaven has become more real than anything else. Glimpsing through these veiled visions, this world and any blessings offered in it seem cheap by comparison. This life is short. What if I spend all my life without perfect sex? Without the money I think is due me? Without the comforts I see others have? Then Jesus has promised a greater fulfilment when he comes with his reward to those who stay faithful.

Once life had become more settled, I thought I was well beyond being tricked or tempted. I had not had a seductive thought toward anyone, male or female, for years. I had learned to cut a thought before it even formed a sentence. If I so much as felt an attraction, I would bring the ensuing thought into captivity and reject it.[28] And to rob power from temptation, I wouldn't keep any secrets from Peter.

I wanted to fill my life with things to look forward to and this was easier working in the industry that I worked in. I could look forward to trips overseas and in particular to the UK and Europe. I had longed to go there almost as much as I had longed to have a baby. Several times my name had been selected, and the trip had been cancelled at the last moment. I had been in the travel industry for twelve years now and had still not visited this part of the world. It may have been a record.

A coach company invited me to visit London and then take one of their regular tours through Europe. It was not to be a typical travel agent's trip: four or five days covering what a tourist might do in ten. There would just be one other agent travelling with me and I would meet her at the airport on the day we left.

The flight over was in business class and before we had reached our destination over 30 hours later, Katie and I were firm friends. I had learned that she was married to a farmer and had no children. She was originally from south London and was hoping to catch up with family after the tour. I was going to visit an uncle in Cambridge.

Katie wanted me to know that she was a very independent traveller and liked to explore at a fast rate. I was the same and was glad she would understand that I would disappear and adventure on my own. We were two of a kind, so much so, that we only did this on our first day in London and after this became inseparable.

Katie had a great sense of humour and after the years of hope and despair over infertility, it was fun to be laughing again. New Zealand was as far away as possible and we were on a tour through the romantic regions of Europe; Paris, Venice, Lucerne and Salzburg were on the itinerary. In New Zealand, it had been winter, dull and gloomy and wet. Suddenly I was in summer and the world was beautiful.

I talked to Katie about Jesus. She was antagonistic but it was obvious that despite my religious side, she liked me. On the coach, people thought we had been friends for decades. She had a handsome face and sparkling dark eyes. I hadn't noticed these until we had been on the road for a week or so, but now I found myself not only noting that we were relaxed together, but also struggling with my old feelings again.

By Venice, I was almost giving way to the arguments that it wouldn't be so bad to leave my life behind. Katie wanted to go on a gondola on the canals and I was all for it. She and I, cruising down the canal with the lights of the houses and restaurants throwing carnival mischief onto the dark water. The gondolier could sing and there was just one seat for us to share. I purified the thought with the memory that I was walking in my father's footsteps since he had been in a gondola in Venice.

My good intent was submerging. The surface thoughts were a bit like the canals of Venice, beautiful and alluring but no one would want to sink into these murky waters or swim in them. I almost prayed, and then was rescued by a deluge of rain. The gondola couldn't go out in this rain; we had to go back to the hotel.

The rooms were problematic. I hadn't known that in Europe it was common to have a twin room where two single beds were together and only separated by the linen! I was literally sharing a bed with Katie with a few inches of bedding to keep me from reaching out to her! My heart would not obey my discipline and I felt myself falling for Katie. Nothing had been said, but the magnetism was as strong as when I first met Sharon. I knew that to say something could sow fatal seeds. I had casually asked her if she had ever had anything to do with gay people but she said she hadn't.

If I was imagining this pull and she was innocent, it would have surprised me. Now we spent every waking moment together and at night, I clung to my side of the bed in fear that I might do something in my sleep!

I tried to remind myself of Pete and the life we had in New Zealand. It was a distant memory. All that mattered was that there were warm summer days and there was Katie. The coach rolled into Lucerne and I had survived another night.

I had walked so much in Venice that for the first time in days, I couldn't go out and about with Katie. I needed to buy some decent walking shoes and the little walking I could do would just get me to the local historic area where I might find a shoe shop. Here I found a small church. I went inside and gratefully noted that there was just one elderly lady, dressed totally in black, sitting in a pew praying. I knelt in a pew and began to cry out to God.

"Lord! I don't want to do this! Please help me!"

That evening we went to the riverside to have coffee. Katie and I sat facing each other and talking. Suddenly I heard the sound of a Christian chorus being sung, in English. The music was drifting across the river from the old part of the town. The song soaked through me like water on dry ground.

"I have to go over there!"

"Why?" grouched Katie.

"Because they're my family!"

"They are NOT your family," she snapped. Her response strengthened my resolve.

"I'm going over."

On the other shore I met a group of YWAM young people sharing their faith and singing. I was astonished to find that few of them spoke any English! With the help of a couple of the English speakers and some of my schoolgirl French, I asked them why they were singing in English.

"We like the sound of the songs in English," they laughed. They gave me a card with a chocolate heart on it, telling me that Jesus loved me. I ate the chocolate, but still have the card! They had saved my spiritual life. From this moment, it was easier.

We returned to London and I went to visit my uncle. He was a dear old chap who had been a headmaster at High Wycombe. He was wonderfully hospitable but I was in turmoil and confusion. I phoned Pete, but I couldn't tell him what had happened as my uncle was there. Peter was having a great time with the young people we led in our church, with good things happening in their lives and as he talked excitedly about these things, I felt a failure and alone.

Back in London, Katie had left me a long and affectionate

letter as we had missed each other by a day at the hotel. I saw her once more when she came to visit my office and Pete was there. He couldn't help but notice that there was something possibly dormant in this girl, and I saw the cool treatment she was giving him.

When I was able to look back over what had happened in Europe, I could see that the Lord had taken me right back to my first failure. The intensity of temptation was just the same but this time I won. I have never had to face this battle again. Having a record of victories where there have been failures in the past is the only way to become stronger and stronger.

Pete was great with the few of my old friends that continued to contact me. At one of the guys' birthday parties many of the guys flirted with him and I learned that their nickname for Pete was "Shirl's sweet man". He had to go to a fortieth birthday party for one of the women, where he found to his relief that there was at least one other bloke. They chatted for hours in the kitchen until I could see that the girls were getting to that hour in drinking, when things could get feisty and nasty and Pete would be a first target, so we left.

On the way home I asked if Pete had enjoyed talking to Don.

"Yeah, he was a great guy." I knew Pete thought Don was a bit of a farm boy as he was not the snappiest of dressers and his beard was not the tidy type the gay guys kept.

"Yep. I didn't want to tell you while we were there, but Don used to be a girl. I knew him when he was Theresa ... "

Pete took it all in his stride and attempted to care for and love any he met. Monica, the girl I had gone to Sydney with, came home from Australia pregnant in the second year of our marriage and I had the privilege of being with her when she had her baby boy.

Once I was Bible bashing Monica and said to her, "Why don't you just give your life to Jesus right now?"

"But I would have to give up my relationship," she replied.

"Who told you that?" I said quite startled.

"Well, I watched what you did and I know what it would mean."

She tolerated my pressure and sermonizing for years. Eventually she made some steps to come to know Jesus and relinquished her life to God. This, and my father returning to a strong relationship with Jesus, just after my mother's death, have been the greatest joys of my life so far!

It was nearly 18 years before I began to tell my story. Amazingly, the first occasion was at the very church in Christchurch where I had been so humiliated and my downward spiral had begun. The pastor was now Peter Hira and his wife Vera was the daughter of the Welsh preacher, Pastor Thomas, whose fiery message had rung in my heart so many years ago in Whangarei: Don't live a half-baked Christian commitment but be done with sin and follow Jesus whatever the cost. At last I was living it!

There was one more major area to tidy up. I had forgiven my parents and thought I had worked through all the hurts of my past and let the harmful things go. Then one Saturday night I had a vision of a huge chain dropping down from the ceiling of our bedroom. I woke with a fright seeing this chain and screamed. Pete stirred from his sleep and muttered a prayer but even as he did, for some reason, I knew that this chain had to do with deep, unspoken hatred that I had continued to harbour against my mother.

My mother's own demons and torments made her a master with verbal knives. It was an ongoing process making sure that each new stab was met with forgiveness. For example, when I showed her the video of my ordination as a minister in 1988 when I received full credentials, she remarked, "What are they clapping for you for?" She often wanted to hear what I preached only to say, "I can't believe people come to hear such rubbish!" Or, "Did you wear THAT outfit? You don't look like the back of a bus in it; you look like the side of one!"

A lot of our surrender to Jesus is the surrender of what we think are our rights. This can be our rights to motherhood, to health, prosperity or on the other scale, our rights to anger and offence. We have no rights. I had no right to hold a grain of hatred for my mother. I let it go. She didn't change, but she could no longer hurt me. She was a Christian but a tormented one. I am not her judge and I look forward to seeing her again in heaven, when we will both be very different!

Our marriage has survived where I have seen many others fail that had perhaps far less to contend with. It is still based on Jesus Christ and relies on his strength. I can't minimize the difficulties that it takes to walk away from homosexuality, but I defy the popular beliefs that say people like me don't exist. I am free, by God's grace, and here I stand!

One flip side to our childlessness has been that I have been available to spread my maternal instinct to nurture others. I have gained many "sons" and "daughters" of many different nationalities.

Maybe your struggle is not with homosexuality or maybe you have had so many failures that you don't dare to think that you can walk free. My prayer is that if you have read my story, and if a light has gone on, and through my experience you are able to tenaciously take hold of wholeness, then you are also my consolation. If I can be a forerunner and you want to run with me, following Jesus no matter the price, you can join an army of overcomers and I too gain another son or daughter in some measure.

Scripture References
(NIV except where noted)

Pervading book: Song of Songs

1. Matthew 18:6–7 But if anyone causes one of these little ones who believe in me to sin, it would be better for him to have a large millstone hung around his neck and to be drowned in the depths of the sea. Woe to the world because of the things that cause people to sin! Such things must come, but woe to the man through whom they come!

2. Romans 6:23 For the wages of sin is death, but the gift of God is eternal life in Christ Jesus our Lord.

3. Colossians 3:22–24 Slaves, obey your earthly masters in everything; and do it, not only when their eye is on you and to win their favour, but with sincerity of heart and reverence for the Lord. Whatever you do, work at it with all your heart, as working for the Lord, not for men.

4. Galatians 6:11 See what large letters I use as I write to you with my own hand!

5. Genesis 3:8 Then the man and his wife heard the sound of the Lord God as he was walking in the garden in the cool of the day, and they hid from the Lord God among the trees of the garden.

6   Matthew 12:39 He answered, "A wicked and adulterous generation asks for a miraculous sign!"

7   Ecclesiastes 2:10 I denied myself nothing my eyes desired; I refused my heart no pleasure.

8   Proverbs 23:29–35 Who has woe? Who has sorrow? Who has strife? Who has complaints? Who has needless bruises? Who has bloodshot eyes? Those who linger over wine, who go to sample bowls of mixed wine. Do not gaze at wine when it is red, when it sparkles in the cup, when it goes down smoothly! In the end it bites like a snake and poisons like a viper. Your eyes will see strange sights and your mind imagine confusing things. You will be like one sleeping on the high seas, lying on top of the rigging. "They hit me," you will say, "but I am not hurt! They beat me, but I don't feel it! When will I wake up so I can find another drink?"

9   Joshua 5:15 The commander of the Lord's army replied, "Take off your sandals, for the place where you are standing is holy."
    Revelation 19:11–14 I saw heaven standing open and there before me was a white horse, whose rider is called Faithful and True. With justice he judges and makes war. His eyes are like blazing fire, and on his head are many crowns. He has a name written on him that no one knows but he himself. He is dressed in a robe dipped in blood, and his name is the Word of God. The armies of heaven were following him, riding on white horses and dressed in fine linen, white and clean.

10 1 Timothy 2:14 And Adam was not the one deceived; it was the woman who was deceived and became a sinner.

1 Corinthians 11:10 For this reason, and because of the angels, the woman ought to have a sign of authority on her head.

11 2 Peter 2:22 Of them the proverbs are true: "A dog returns to its vomit," and, "A sow that is washed goes back to her wallowing in the mud."

12 Jeremiah 1:5 Before I formed you in the womb I knew you, before you were born I set you apart; I appointed you as a prophet to the nations.

13 1 Corinthians 1:27 But God chose the foolish things of the world to shame the wise; God chose the weak things of the world to shame the strong.

14 Daniel 1:8 But Daniel resolved not to defile himself with the royal food and wine.

15 Psalms 37:4 Delight yourself in the Lord and he will give you the desires of your heart.

16 1 Corinthians 6:17 But he that is joined unto the Lord is one spirit. (King James Version)

17 Psalm 141:5 Let a righteous man strike me – it is a kindness; let him rebuke me – it is oil on my head. My head will not refuse it.

18 Acts 19:13–16 Some Jews who went around driving out evil spirits tried to invoke the name of the Lord Jesus over those who were demon-possessed. They would say, "In the name of Jesus, whom Paul preaches, I command you to come out." Seven sons of Sceva, a Jewish chief priest, were

doing this. One day the evil spirit answered them, "Jesus I know, and I know about Paul, but who are you?" Then the man who had the evil spirit jumped on them and over-powered them all. He gave them such a beating that they ran out of the house naked and bleeding.

19 Leviticus 26:8 Five of you will chase a hundred, and a hundred of you will chase ten thousand, and your enemies will fall by the sword before you.

20 1 Corinthians 14:35 If they want to enquire about something, they should ask their own husbands at home.

21 Luke 1:37 For nothing is impossible with God.

22 Luke 4:24 "I tell you the truth," he continued, "no prophet is accepted in his home town."

23 Haggai 2:10 and 19 On the twenty-fourth day of the ninth month, in the second year of Darius, the word of the Lord came to the prophet Haggai: ... "Until now, the vine and the fig-tree, the pomegranate and the olive tree have not borne fruit. From this day on I will bless you."

24 Ruth 1:16 But Ruth replied, "Don't urge me to leave you or to turn back from you. Where you go I will go, and where you stay I will stay. Your people will be my people and your God my God."

25 Ephesians 5:33 ... and the wife must respect her husband.

26 Ephesians 5:25 Husbands, love your wives, just as Christ loved the church and gave himself up for her to make her holy.

27 1 Samuel 1:15–16 "I am a woman who is deeply troubled. I have not been drinking wine or beer; I was pouring out my soul to the Lord. Do not take your servant for a wicked woman; I have been praying here out of my great anguish and grief."

28 2 Corinthians 10:5 ... we take captive every thought to make it obedient to Christ.